IN THESE LAST DAYS
The Message of Hebrews

Other Books by Félix H. Cortez

Within the Veil: The Ascension of the Son in the Letter to the Hebrews

"Did You Know . . . ?": Stories and Anecdotes to Rev Up Your Life

IN THESE LAST DAYS

The Message of Hebrews

Félix H. Cortez

Pacific Press®
Publishing Association

Nampa, Idaho | www.pacificpress.com

Additional copies of this book are available for purchase by calling toll-free 1-800-765-6955 or by visiting AdventistBookCenter.com.

Library of Congress Cataloging-in-Publication Data

Names: Cortez, Félix H., author.
Title: In these last days : the message of Hebrews / Félix H. Cortez.
Description: Nampa, Idaho : Pacific Press Publishing Association, 2021. |
Summary: "In These Last Days discusses how the New Testament book of Hebrews brought early Christian believers a fresh understanding of Jesus' high priest ministry in the heavenly sanctuary. It also shows how this deeper understanding of Christ's ongoing ministry strengthened their commitment to Him and their witness to the world"— Provided by publisher.
Identifiers: LCCN 2021020444 (print) | LCCN 2021020445 (ebook) | ISBN 9780816367344 | ISBN 9780816367351 (ebook)
Subjects: LCSH: Bible. Hebrews—Criticism, interpretation, etc.
Classification: LCC BS2775.52 .C67 2021 (print) | LCC BS2775.52 (ebook) | DDC 227/.8706—dc23
LC record available at https://lccn.loc.gov/2021020444
LC ebook record available at https://lccn.loc.gov/2021020445

July 2021

Dedication

To Alma G., Hadid J., and Alma N.,
with love and admiration.

Contents

Introduction

Like a precious gem, Hebrews is rare, enigmatic, and exceptional. On the one hand, Hebrews contains important theological exposi- tions. Its teaching about Christ is profound, including penetrating insights about His humanity and divinity (Hebrews 1; 2). It also provides a careful analysis of the meaning of the New Covenant and the roles of the law and the cross in our salvation (Hebrews 8–10). More importantly, however, Hebrews contains distinctive theologi- cal contributions that are especially significant for Adventists. It provides the most extended explanation in the New Testament of the meaning of the Sabbath and its observance (Hebrews 3; 4), explains in detail Jesus' priestly ministry in the heavenly sanctuary (Hebrews 5–10), and contains robust instruction and probably the most famous affirmation in the New Testament about the creation of the universe (Hebrews 11:3). Thus, together with Daniel, Revela- tion, Leviticus, and Genesis, Hebrews is especially valuable for Adventist theology

On the other hand, the exhortations of Hebrews are profoundly moving. While its warnings against apostasy are sobering,[1] its descrip- tion of Jesus as the anchor of our hope is reassuring and comforting.[2]

It also contains one of the most emotive calls to faith and perseverance in Scripture.[3]

The mystery of Hebrews

Hebrews is a rare document. Though sent as a letter, it was probably not intended as one. Instead, the author describes the document as a "word of exhortation," which was the expression that was used to refer to a sermon in both the synagogue and the Christian church.[4] Accordingly, it describes the author as a speaker, not as a writer.[5] Thus, it is often pointed out that Hebrews "is the most elegant and sophisticated, and perhaps the most enigmatic, text of first-century Christianity . . . a masterpiece of early Christian rhetorical homiletics."[6]

Hebrews is also enigmatic. After almost two millennia of study, scholars do not agree on the answers to six important questions: Who wrote it? To whom was it written? When was it written? Is it a letter or a sermon? What is its literary structure? And how should we understand its symbolic language?

Hebrews was probably written by the apostle Paul from Rome between the years AD 60 and 65 to Hellenist Jewish Christians living in Jerusalem.[7] We know the author was male because he uses the Greek masculine participle *diēgoumenon* ("to tell") in Hebrews 11:32 when referring to himself. We also know that he was possibly in jail when he wrote, as his movements were restricted (Hebrews 13:18, 19).[8] He also refers to Timothy, and the only Timothy we know from early Christian sources was the companion of Paul (verse 23). The kinds of topics and images that the author chooses suggest that he was probably of Jewish origin. Likewise, his argumentation is closer to Jewish midrash than to other systems of reasoning.[9] He was also presumably well educated and enjoyed rhetorical training.

Most importantly, Hebrews always appears in New Testament manuscripts as part of the Pauline letter collection. The Chester Beatty papyrus P[46]—the earliest manuscript of Hebrews and of the Pauline letters—places Hebrews right after Romans. Hebrews already bears the title "To [the] Hebrews," which follows the way Pauline letters were identified and is different from the way catholic epistles were identified. The question that remains, then, is why did Paul, or the author, not identify himself? We know that the audience knew who the author was (verses 8, 19). Was Paul trying to protect the addressees from persecution, as some have suggested?[10]

Hebrews was written from Rome. Paul includes the greetings of the Italians, who are with him, as was the custom in the early Christian churches.[11] This greeting suggests that Paul wrote Hebrews between AD 60, the time he first arrived in Rome, and around AD 65, when he died there, according to tradition.

Paul is probably writing to a home church of Hellenist Jewish Christians in Jerusalem—that is, Jewish Christians whose first language was Greek and had been born outside Palestine. The readers may have moved to Jerusalem to receive further education, as Paul himself had done, or, perhaps in other cases, to participate in establishing the Messianic kingdom.[12] Thus, the author distinguishes his readers from their leaders as well as from other Christians in the area (verses 17, 24). It is also possible that Paul knew at least some of them from the time when he lived in Jerusalem before his conversion (Acts 6:1–8:1).

The argument of Hebrews suggests that the audience of Hebrews had a problem of double allegiance. They had difficulty understanding the meaning and implications of Jesus' priestly ministry in the heavenly sanctuary (Hebrews 5:11–6:8). They were slow to recognize that Jesus' death, ascension, and ministry in the heavenly sanctuary had made obsolete the Levitical priesthood, the temple, and the sacrifices of animals.[13] They were Jewish Christians who, though having accepted Jesus in the past, remained loyal to the Jerusalem temple and its rituals. Acts provides evidence that Jewish believers continued to offer sacrifices many years after the death and ascension of Jesus (Acts 21:23, 24). Hebrews argues that such sacrifices were obsolete and soon to disappear and that their offering should not continue.[14] In fact, the author suggests that continuing to offer these sacrifices could eventually lead to the rejection of Jesus and His sacrifice (Hebrews 6:4–6; 10:26–29).

Hebrews is the third-longest letter of Paul.[15] Considering the amount of papyrus used, the cost of the secretary, the production of the letter to be sent, and the copy to be retained by the author, E. Randolph Richards has calculated that the author spent at least the equivalent of US$2,000.[16] This amount did not include the costs of a messenger. If Paul was a prisoner when he produced this letter, what kind of sacrifices and fundraising must it have taken to write and send it? I think Paul wrote this letter because he thought it was important and deserved his investment and sacrifice.

In these last days

The first assertion of the author, and probably the most important, was that "in these last days [God] has spoken to us in His Son" (Hebrews 1:2, NASB). The readers of Hebrews did not know it yet, but their world was going to end within the next ten years. The meltdown of Jerusalem and Jewish society would be epic and tragic, like the Flood and the fall of Babylon, a time of trouble as the world had not yet seen (Matthew 24:21, 22). They sensed, however, that the end was approaching fast.

The signs that the end was approaching were increasing in number and intensity. The clouds began to gather with the ascension of Gaius—whom the soldiers called Caligula—in AD 37. The following year the Jews of Alexandria suffered pogroms that culminated with the public scourging of thirty-eight Jewish elders on August 31.[17]

Around two years later, offended that a Jew had pulled down an altar to him in the city of Jamnia, Gaius ordered the legate of Syria, Publius Petronius, to set up a gigantic statue of him in the temple in Jerusalem. This order threatened to trigger the worst crisis since the desecration of the temple by Antiochus Epiphanes (167–164 BC). It surely reminded the followers of Jesus of His prediction less than ten years earlier that an "abomination of desolation" would stand in the

Holy Place (Matthew 24:15; Mark 13:14). Fortunately, Gaius was assassinated on January 24, AD 41, before the order could be carried out.[18] Paul most likely alluded to this event around ten years later when he suggested that Gaius's attempt to set up his statue in the temple in Jerusalem prefigured what the man of lawlessness would later do in the temple of God (2 Thessalonians 2:3, 4).

In AD 41, Claudius forbade Jews in Rome to gather together "in accordance with their ancestral way of life."[19] Eight years later (AD 49), Claudius expelled them from Rome due to the constant riots at the instigation of a certain Chrestus,[20] which, some scholars think, may have been a mistaken reference to Christ, suggesting that the disturbances were caused by conflicts between Jews and Christians.[21]

From AD 46 to 48, a famine hit Palestine and the surrounding territories. Agabus, a Christian prophet, predicted this famine, and Christians from Antioch sent relief to Christians in Jerusalem through Barnabas and Paul (Acts 11:27–30). The famine, aggravated by high taxes, the oppression of the Roman occupation, and the extreme polarization between the rich and the poor, frayed the social fabric. Josephus notes that a false prophet named Theudas arose in Palestine around that time.[22] He convinced many people to take their property and follow him into the wilderness across the Jordan River, which, at his command, would divide as Joshua had parted the waters of the Jordan before. The plan seemed to be that God would prepare them in the desert for the new conquest of Palestine. But Cuspius Fadus, the Roman procurator, dispersed the movement, executed Theudas, and exhibited his head in Jerusalem.[23] About ten years later (ca. AD 55), a Jewish prophet known as the Egyptian (Acts 21:38) invited his followers to march from the wilderness to the Mount of Olives and then into Jerusalem. Felix, the Roman governor, slaughtered many of them and scattered the movement.[24] Still, there would be many others like them.

By AD 59, the time of Paul's last travel to Jerusalem recorded in the Bible, Palestine was in turmoil. According to Tacitus, Felix, the governor, "practiced every kind of cruelty and lust."[25] The high priest was Ismael ben Phiabi II, a thug. An ancient lament bemoaned, "Woe is me because of the house of Ishmael b. Phiabi, woe is me because of their thuggery! For they are high priests, and their sons, treasures [*sic*], their sons-in-law trustees, and their slaves beat up on the people with clubs" (b. Pesah. 57a).[26] No wonder that Paul, as he prepared to travel, requested prayers that he might be delivered from the unbelievers in Judea (Romans 15:31).

Hebrews was probably written around AD 62, toward the end of Paul's first imprisonment in Rome. That same year, James, the brother of Jesus and leader of the church in Jerusalem, was assassinated by the temple authorities. When Porcius Festus had suddenly died while in office, the high priest Annas the younger, whom Josephus describes as an insolent man, saw an opportunity. He convened the Sanhedrin, accused James of breaking the law, and condemned him to be stoned to death, which he would not have had the power to do had there been a Roman governor in office.[27]

Josephus tells us that there were many foreboding signs of the fall of Jerusalem. He especially relates that during the Feast of Tabernacles that same year (AD 62), a certain Jesus, son of Ananias, an untrained peasant, stood up in the temple and began to cry: "A voice from the east, a voice from the west, a voice from the four winds, a voice against Jerusalem and the holy house, a voice against the bridegrooms and the brides, and a voice against this whole people!"[28] He continued to cry this warning taken from Jeremiah's temple sermon (Jeremiah 7:34) for seven years and five months, despite beatings and floggings by the authorities, until he died in AD 69 during the siege of Jerusalem.

Jewish society had begun to unravel. It was probably around this time that Hellenistic believers in Jerusalem received Paul's letter about Jesus, the Son, seated at the right hand of God, a powerful and merciful Priest interceding in their behalf in a time of need.

As I write these words, our world and society also seem to be on the brink. COVID-19 has disrupted our world, and natural disasters seem to be increasing in number and destructive power. Society is fraying, and political systems around the globe are becoming increasingly polarized and unstable. Seasoned thinkers and observers have begun to express their fears that democracy itself is in peril.

These circumstances make us realize that we also need a fresh view of the Son of God, the powerful Ruler and Intercessor who sits at the right hand of God. May God open our eyes to a clearer and deeper vision of Jesus as we study this letter for the last days.

---

1. Hebrews 6:1–8.

2. Hebrews 10:19–25.

3. Hebrews 10:35–12:4.

4. Hebrews 13:22; cf. Acts 13:15; 1 Timothy 4:13.

5. Hebrews 8:1; cf. 2:5; 5:11; 6:9; 11:32; cf. 9:5.

6. Harold W. Attridge, *The Epistle to the Hebrews* (Philadelphia: Fortress, 1989), 1.

7. See Félix H. Cortez, *The Letter to the Hebrews*, Seventh-day Adventist International Bible Commentary (Nampa, ID: Pacific Press®, forthcoming).

8. Another possibility is that he was sick.

9. See Daniel Boyarin, "Midrash in Hebrews, Hebrews as Midrash," in *Hebrews in Contexts* (Boston: Brill, 2016), 15–30.

10. E.g., Christos Sp. Voulgaris, "Hebrews: Paul's Fifth Epistle From Prison," *Greek Orthodox Theological Review* 44 (1999): 200; David L. Allen, *Hebrews*, New American Commentary (Nashville: B & H, 2010), 66–68.

11. 1 Corinthians 16:8, 19; Philippians 4:22; Titus 3:15; 1 Peter 5:13; 3 John 14.

12. E.g., Isaiah 11:10–12:6; 40:9–11; Jeremiah 31:10–12; Ezekiel 34:11–31; cf. Acts 1:6.

13. Priesthood: Hebrews 7:11–28; temple: Hebrews 8:1, 2, 5; 9:11, 12, 23, 24; sacrifices of animals: Hebrews 8:3, 4; 9:9, 10; 10:1–4, 11–14, 18.

14. Hebrews 8:13; 9:9, 10; 10:1–4, 18.

15. After Romans and 1 Corinthians.

16. E. Randolph Richards, *Paul and First-Century Letter Writing: Secretaries, Composition, and Collections* (Downers Grove, IL: InterVarsity, 2004), 165–169.

17. F. F. Bruce, *New Testament History* (New York: Doubleday, 1969), 252.

18. Bruce, 253–258.

19. Bruce, 295.

20. Suetonius, *Divus Claudius* 25.4.

21. Bruce, *New Testament History*, 297, 298.

22. This Theudas may be different from the one mentioned in Acts 5:36.

23. Josephus, *Jewish Antiquities* 20.5.1.

24. Acts 21:38; Josephus, *Jewish Antiquities* 20.8.6; Josephus, *Jewish War* 2.13.5.

25. Tacitus, *Historiae* 5.10

26. Jacob Neusner, *The Babylonian Talmud: A Translation and Commentary* (Peabody, MA: Hendrickson, 2011), 4:256.

27. Josephus, *Jewish Antiquities* 20.9.1; Bruce, *New Testament History*, 368–377.

28. Josephus, *Jewish War* 6.5.3.

One

The Letter to the Hebrews and to Us

The Boston Marathon is the world's oldest annual marathon competition and one of the most important and prestigious road races in the world today. Until the COVID pandemic in 2020, it had been run without interruption since 1897, attracting around thirty thousand registered participants and five hundred thousand spectators every year. It is one of the World Marathon Majors[1] and is among the most difficult marathons in the world. One of the main reasons for its difficulty is the four "Newton Hills," the last of which is known as Heartbreak Hill. These hills are not very large, but they are located at a crucial moment in the race, between miles 17 and 21, five miles before the end.[2] The race begins downhill for the first five miles, and then the terrain is mostly flat for a while. The Newton Hills come in the last third of the race when the glycogen stored in the muscles is most likely depleted, triggering pain and extreme fatigue in the runners. The last hill is not high, only eighty-eight feet, but the accumulation of ascents and fatigue pushes runners to the brink. Marathoners call the extreme exhaustion many feel at this point of the race "hitting the wall." It is at this moment that many less-fit runners abandon the race.

The Christian experience cycle

The story of the letter to the Hebrews tells us that the audience was at a similar point of fatigue in the race of Christian life. The story of the congregation began when the good news about Jesus was preached to them. We do not know who the original evangelists were, but we do know that God Himself confirmed their testimony through "signs and wonders and various miracles and by gifts of the Holy Spirit distributed according to his will" (Hebrews 2:4). The New Testament relates that signs[3] like miraculous healings, exorcisms,[4] and outpouring of spiritual gifts[5] often accompanied the preaching of the gospel in new places. If the audience lived in Jerusalem, it is possible that they had experienced the powerful manifestations of the Holy Spirit in the time of the Pentecost or during the subsequent years. They must have been filled as well with the Holy Spirit. The author suggests that they had "tasted the heavenly gift, and . . . shared in the Holy Spirit, and . . . tasted the goodness of the word of God and the powers of the age to come" (Hebrews 6:4, 5). It must have been a thrilling experience. They probably also participated in the selfless sharing of goods with less fortunate believers (Acts 4:32–37). In fact, the author says that they had served the saints and still did (Hebrews 6:10).

But the powerful beginning of the gospel was followed by persecution. The author of Hebrews says that they were publicly exposed to persecution and affliction, that some of them were mistreated and put into jail, and that their property was plundered (Hebrews 10:32–34; 13:1–3). This could have been the result of the actions of mobs, the official seizure of houses and property, or the imposition of heavy fines. The Hebrews account fits well with Luke's description of persecution in Palestine and Jerusalem.[6] The author describes the persecution as public exposure to "reproach" (the Greek term *oneidismos* refers to verbal aggressions on honor and character). Cultural anthropologists have noted that there is a close relationship between a person's honor and the treatment of his or her body. It is also possible that they were accused of grave crimes. A couple of years later, Nero would accuse the Christians living in Rome of starting the fire that devastated Rome in the summer of AD 64.[7] Similarly, the historian Tacitus considered them guilty of "hatred against humanity."[8] Suetonius, another historian, mentions that they were accused of promoting "a new and mischievous superstition."[9] We also know that Christians would later be slandered with cannibalism (the Lord's Supper), atheism (rejection of pagan gods), incest (Christians called each other "brother," "sister"), and superstitious beliefs (e.g., the end of the world).[10]

The audience of Hebrews valiantly endured the abuses and sufferings for the name of Christ (Hebrews 10:32–34), but now a sense of fatigue and malaise had taken hold. They had begun to "drift away" from Christ (Hebrews 2:1). Some began to neglect the meetings of the church (Hebrews 10:25). Hospitality and care for those in prison began to fail (Hebrews 13:1, 2), and a root of bitterness and unbelief threatened to grow in the hearts of some (Hebrews 12:15; 3:12). They were spiritually exhausted. There is something glorious in a climactic fight for one's faith in the face of daunting odds, in the midst of attacks against our Savior. A protracted fight against suffering and disappointment is more difficult. Thus, it has been remarked that it is easier to die as a martyr than to live as a saint. The audience had responded gloriously to persecution in years past, but now they were dealing with the ignominy of poverty and the disgrace of prolonged imprisonment.

I cannot forget that sunny summer day when a mother asked me to say something to help her son. I had been invited to preach at the Pathfinder camporee of a large union, and the mother had attended, seeking help. She explained that her husband had been kidnapped many months before and that they did not know anything about him, not even whether he was dead or alive. Her son, once very active in the church, did not want to go to church anymore or read his Bible. "Pastor," she implored, "please speak with him." I wondered how many prayers by that young child had gone unheard. I do not remember their names, but I still pray for them. Did God reach him with His mighty arm as He reached my son? I wish I knew.

Hebrews was written for a congregation whose memory of the glorious signs and wonders of the Lord were part of a past that was quickly receding. It was written for a congregation that was at the border of the Promised Land,[11] the moment of the race where there is fatigue, where the enthusiasm of the beginning of the race has become drudgery, and the finish line seems just out of reach. The last stretch has always been a moment of danger for the people of God. It was at Kadesh, the border of the Promised Land, where Israel lost faith after the cowering report of the ten spies (Numbers 13; 14). It was in Kadesh again, almost forty years later, where Moses and Aaron lost their patience, struck the rock, and were forbidden to enter into the Promised Land (Numbers 20). It was at Peor, right beside the Jordan, where the people engaged in idolatry and immorality and a great number were destroyed (Numbers 25). In the last stretch of the race, our senses become dull; we lose focus and are prone to commit grievous mistakes. Runners often say that a marathon has two halves, the first 20 miles and the last 6.2. Or a marathon is a 6.2-mile race with a 20-mile warm-up.

The letter to the Hebrews was written as a word of exhortation to help the audience successfully run the last stretch of the race. The author does three things to achieve this purpose: he redirects their attention to Jesus, exhorts them to have faith, and urges them to work for one another.[12]

The "word of exhortation"

There are two kinds of material in the letter to the Hebrews: theological arguments and exhortatory appeals.[13] Today scholars and students focus mainly on the rich theological exposition of the letter, but the author considered the letter to be a "word of exhortation" (Hebrews 13:22). This suggests, then, that the theological argumentation the author provides in the letter has the purpose of establishing the foundation for his appeal to the audience.

The exhortatory appeal of the author is summarized two times in the letter: Hebrews 4:14–16 and Hebrews 10:19–25. These two paragraphs are the most important markers of the structure of Hebrews and function as do the twin towers of San Francisco's Golden Gate Bridge; they summarize and support the argument of the letter as a whole.[14] They divide Hebrews into three great sections: Hebrews 1–4 focuses on Jesus' intercession at the right hand of God as King and Priest. Hebrews 5–10 focuses on Jesus' priesthood according to the order of Melchizedek (chapters 5–7) and the new covenant He has inaugurated through His sacrifice (chapters 8–10). Hebrews 11–13 is a call to faith and perseverance (chapters 11; 12) and to work for one another in brotherly love (chapter 13).

The first clause in both paragraphs (Hebrews 4:14–16; 10:19–25) provides a summary of the theological points made in the previous section and is introduced by the expression "therefore, since . . ." (NASB). Hebrews 4:14–16 focuses on the fact that Jesus lived a sinless life, "passed through the heavens" (verse 14), and sits at the right hand of God as Ruler and High Priest on our behalf. This is the argument of Hebrews 1–4. This theological fact becomes, then, the basis for the exhortation, "Let us hold fast our confession" and "let us draw near with confidence to the throne of grace" (Hebrews 4:14, 16, NASB). Thus, the powerful theological fact that Jesus ascended to the right hand of God as our King and High Priest is the basis for the exhortation to "draw near" in faith and prayer.

Similarly, Hebrews 10:19–25 focuses on two theological facts. The first fact is that Jesus has opened for us "a new and living way . . . through the veil" (verse 20, NASB). The author is referring to the new covenant Jesus inaugurated through His blood, which provides us with confident access to the presence of God because of the forgiveness it provides. This is a summary of the arguments of Hebrews 8–10. The second fact is that Jesus is a Great High Priest over the house of God (Hebrews 10:21). This is a summary of Hebrews 5–7, which describes Jesus' priesthood according to the order of Melchizedek. These two powerful theological facts provide the basis for three exhortations.

First, "Let us draw near with a sincere heart" (Hebrews 10:22, NASB). This is an invitation to confident prayer because of the forgiveness or cleansing Jesus has provided. Second, "Let us hold fast the confession of our hope" (verse 23). This is again an exhortation to faith. Finally, "Let us consider how to stimulate one another to love and good deeds" (verse 24, NASB). This is an exhortation to work for one another.

Therefore, the strategy of the author of Hebrews to address the spiritual fatigue of his audience has three elements. The first element is that the author refocuses the attention of the audience on the person and work of Jesus Christ. He knows that if the audience is going to successfully complete their race, they need to fix their eyes on Jesus (Hebrews 12:1, 2). He does this with a fresh analysis of Jesus' achievements. But he does not simply repeat the points made by other early Christian authors.

The letter of Hebrews is unique in its deep analysis of the priesthood of Jesus. As the fight for Christian life continues, Christians need an ever-deepening understanding of who Jesus is. Repetition is not enough. This was the problem that plagued the readers of Hebrews; they had remained content with understanding only "the elementary principles of the oracles of God" (Hebrews 5:12, NASB). That is why they were sliding little by little toward apostasy (Hebrews 5:11–6:8, NASB).

A deeper theological understanding of Jesus, however, is not enough. We need an ever-deepening commitment. We need to hold fast to faith. But, similarly, faith is not enough. Faith needs to ask in prayer. The believer needs to "draw near with confidence" and with "a sincere heart" (Hebrews 4:16; 10:22, NASB).

Finally, even prayer alone is not enough. The believer needs to work for others. The author of Hebrews teaches that the main reason to attend church meetings is not to learn more or to receive encouragement. The main reason to attend church meetings is to help others, encourage others, and work for others.[15] In the process of doing that, we are encouraged, and we obtain a deeper insight into Christ.

22

In the end, spiritual fatigue results from a tendency to focus on ourselves—our suffering, our loneliness, our failure, our inadequacy, and our weakness. When the angel met a depressed Elijah in the desert, the only thing the disheartened prophet could think about was that he was not better than his fathers, that he had failed to enact the reforms he desired, and that he was the only one faithful in Israel. But then, God gave Elijah a deeper insight into who He is and sent him back to work (1 Kings 19).

As we near the end of the race, we cannot lose our focus. We need to obtain a deeper understanding of who Jesus is, confirm our faith, and renew our work for others. As we do this, we will be strengthened to finish the course.

---

1. The other five are in Tokyo, London, Berlin, Chicago, and New York City.

2. See "Boston Marathon Course Tips for Runners," *Runner's World*, May 14, 2007, https://www.runnersworld.com/races-places/a20790076/boston-marathon-course-tips-for-runners/.

3. Acts 2:43; 5:12; 6:8; 8:13; Romans 15:19; 2 Corinthians 12:12.

4. Acts 3:1–10; 5:16; 9:32–42; 14:8–18; 16:16–18; 19:11, 12.

5. Acts 2:1–11; 4:31; 8:14–25; 10:44–48; 19:1–7; 1 Corinthians 12–14.

6. Acts 4:1–22; 5:17–42; 6:8–8:3; 9:23–29; 12:1–19, etc.

7. Tacitus, *Annals* 15.38–44; Suetonius, *Nero* 38.2; Dio Cassius, *Roman History*, trans. Earnest Cary, vol. 8, Loeb Classical Library 176 (Cambridge, MA: Harvard University, 1925), 74, 75 [62.18.2].

8. Tacitus, *Annals* 15.44.2.

9. Suetonius, *Nero* 16.

10. See D. S. Potter, "Persecution of the Early Church," in *Anchor Bible Dictionary*, ed. David Noel Freedman (New York: Doubleday, 1992), 5:234.

11. Hebrews 10:35–39; 11:39, 40; 1:2; 9:26.

12. Similarly, Ellen G. White says that "for the disheartened there is sure remedy—faith, prayer, work." *Prophets and Kings* (Mountain View, CA: Pacific Press®, 1917), 164, 165.

13. Introduction: Hebrews 1:1–4. Exhortatory appeals: Hebrews 2:1–4; 3:1–4:16; 5:11–6:20; 10:19–13:19. Theological exposition: Hebrews 1:5–14; 2:5–18; 5:1–10; 7:1–10:18. Conclusion: Hebrews 13:20–25.

14. Hebrews 8:1 is a summary of the theological exposition of the letter.

15. Hebrews 10:24, 25; cf. 3:13; 13:15, 16.

Two

The Message of Hebrews

A few years ago, my sister-in-law was walking home from one of our universities where she worked. Arriving at the gate to leave the campus, she felt a strong impression, like a voice, telling her she needed to give her paper-bag lunch to the young person guarding the gate. Unsure of what to do, she continued walking and exited through the gate, but the voice became more insistent and louder, "Give him your lunch!"

"OK, OK," my sister-in-law said, "I am going to do it." She promptly returned to the gate and gave the young man her lunch. Though she never learned the reason for this impression, she was willing to act on the voice she heard.

Have you ever imagined what it would be like to hear God speaking directly to you? What an awesome privilege and responsibility! For the author of Hebrews, the idea of God speaking with people was not a far-fetched notion. "Long ago, at many times and in many ways, God spoke to our fathers by the prophets, but in these last days he has spoken to us *by* his Son" (Hebrews 1:1, 2; emphasis added). The idea is simple. Jesus is the last and the greatest messenger God has used to speak to us. He is the culmination of God's attempts to communicate

His message of salvation to us. Thus, the author emphasizes throughout the letter that we need to pay attention to the message He has communicated through the Son.[1]

But the Greek preposition *en*, translated *by* in the ESV, can also be translated as "to" or "in." Thus, the NASB reads, "In these last days [God] has spoken to us *in* His Son." In this translation, Jesus is not the messenger but *the message*. The issue is fascinating because this translation requires a different kind of response from us. More than hearing what Jesus says, we need to observe who He is and what He does. And more importantly, if Jesus is God's message, then God's message is untranslatable and irreducible. God's message can only be experienced personally, and this experience is nontransferable. We may promote it and recommend it, but in the end, God's message requires a personal relationship with Jesus.

The general argument of the letter suggests that the author is telling us that Jesus is more than the messenger—He *is* the message; He *is* the "word of God" (Hebrews 4:12). This principle will guide our study as we seek to understand the message of Hebrews.

The family dialogue

A peculiar characteristic of Hebrews is that the author describes God as speaking directly to the audience. Pamela Michelle Eisenbaum has noted that almost all of the quotations from the Old Testament "are quotations of *direct speech*."[2] Whether Hebrews quotes the oracles of the prophets or the meditations of the psalmist, the author of Hebrews understands and presents them as if God were speaking the words Himself. The "word of God" is spoken, not written.

This leads to the second distinguishing characteristic of the use of Scripture in Hebrews. The quotations in Hebrews are not used to refer to or evoke something God said in the past; rather, they "re-present" God's words of the past to the audience in the present. They speak "directly to and within the new context" of the audience.[3] In this sense, they are a new speech act of God. This immediacy of the Word of God in Hebrews is important for its exhortatory purpose. Using the quotation of Scripture as God's direct speech, Hebrews constructs through Scripture a world where the readers—or hearers—stand in the presence of God and hear Him speak.

Careful attention to the quotations of Hebrews shows a pattern, a logic, that provides a surprising and beautiful substructure to the argument of Hebrews. The quotations in Hebrews describe a dialogue between the Father, the Son, the Holy Spirit, and the children. Let us focus briefly on the basic text of this family dialogue. I will quote the first cycle of the dialogue and summarize the second, but you can analyze it further in your own Bible.

The Father speaks to the Son
(The enthronement of Christ)

For to which of the angels did *God ever say*, "You are my Son, today I have begotten you"? (Hebrews 1:5, quoting Psalm 2:7).

Or again *[God said]*, "I will be to him a father, and he shall be to me a son"? (Hebrews 1:5, quoting 2 Samuel 7:14).

. . . When he brings the firstborn into the world, *he [God] says*, "Let all God's angels worship him" (Hebrews 1:6, quoting Deuteronomy 32:43, LXX; Psalm 97:7, LXX).

Of the angels *he [God] says*, "He makes his angels winds, and his ministers a flame of fire" (Hebrews 1:7, quoting Psalm 104:4).

But of the Son *he [God] says*,

"Your throne, O God, is forever and ever,
    the scepter of uprightness is the scepter of your kingdom.
You have loved righteousness and hated wickedness;

therefore God, your God, has anointed you
    with the oil of gladness beyond your companions" (Hebrews
       1:8, 9, quoting Psalm 45:6, 7).

And *[God continues saying]*,

"You, Lord, laid the foundation of the earth in the beginning,
    and the heavens are the work of your hands;
they will perish, but you remain;
    they will all wear out like a garment,
like a robe you will roll them up,
    like a garment they will be changed.
But you are the same,
    and your years will have no end" (Hebrews 1:10–12, quoting
       Psalm 102:25–27).

And to which of the angels has *he [God] ever said,* "Sit at my right
hand until I make your enemies a footstool for your feet"?
(Hebrews 1:13, quoting Psalm 110:1).

The Son speaks to the Father
(The faithfulness of the Son)

He [the Son] is not ashamed to call them brethren, saying, "I will
proclaim Your name to My brethren" (Hebrews 2:11b, 12,
NASB, quoting Psalm 22:22).

And again *[the Son says],* "I will put my trust in him" (Hebrews
2:13, quoting 2 Samuel 22:3).

And again *[the Son continues saying],* "Behold, I and the children
God has given me" (Hebrews 2:13, quoting Isaiah 8:18).

The Holy Spirit speaks to the children
(It is time to enter into the rest)

Therefore, as the *Holy Spirit says,*

> "Today, if you hear his voice,
> do not harden your hearts as in the rebellion,
>   on the day of testing in the wilderness,
> where your fathers put me to the test
>   and saw my works for forty years.
> Therefore I was provoked with that generation,
> and said, 'They always go astray in their heart;
>   they have not known my ways.'
> As I swore in my wrath,
>   'They shall not enter my rest' " (Hebrews 3:7–11, quoting
>   Psalm 95:7–11).

The Father speaks to the Son
(The appointment of the Son as High Priest)

"You are my Son, today I have begotten you" (Hebrews 5:5, quoting
   Psalm 2:7).

"You are a priest forever, after the order of Melchizedek" (Hebrews
   5:6, quoting Psalm 110:4).

"You are a priest forever" (Hebrews 7:21, quoting Psalm 110:4).

"Behold, the days are coming, declares the Lord, when I will establish a new covenant with the house of Israel and with the house
   of Judah" (Hebrews 8:8, quoting Jeremiah 31:31 [Jeremiah
   38:31–34, LXX]).

The Son speaks to the Father
(The faithfulness of the Son)

"Behold, I have come to do your will, O God, as it is written of me in the scroll of the book" (Hebrews 10:7, quoting Psalm 40:7, 8).

The Holy Spirit speaks to the children
(God has provided forgiveness of sin)

"I will remember their sins and their lawless deeds no more" (Hebrews 10:17, quoting Jeremiah 31:34).

The Father speaks to the children
(Persevere, hold fast)

"Vengeance is mine; I will repay.". . . "The Lord will judge His people" (Hebrews 10:30, quoting Deuteronomy 32:35, 36).[4]

"Yet a little while,
    and the coming one will come and will not delay;
but my righteous one shall live by faith,
    and if he shrinks back,
my soul has no pleasure in him" (Hebrews 10:37, 38, quoting Isaiah 26:20, 21; Habakkuk 2:3, 4).

"My son, do not regard lightly the discipline of the Lord, nor be weary when reproved by him" (Hebrews 12:5, quoting Proverbs 3:11).

"Yet once more I will shake not only the earth but also the heavens" (Hebrews 12:26, quoting Haggai 2:6).

"I will never leave you nor forsake you" (Hebrews 13:5, quoting Deuteronomy 31:6, 8).

The children to the Father
(Expression of faith)

"The Lord is my helper; I will not fear; what can man do to me?"
(Hebrews 13:6, quoting Psalm 118:6 [Psalm 117:6, LXX]).

It is important to note the following characteristics of this dialogue. First, the dialogue is interesting because the Father speaks to the Son, then the Son responds to the Father, and then the Holy Spirit speaks to the children. This dynamic occurs twice. After the second cycle comes a final cycle in which God speaks directly to the children. Thus, God speaks, Jesus is our Representative, and the Holy Spirit is the Interpreter. The Trinity works as a team for our salvation. Notice that the children are silent, except at the end of the book. It is clear, however, that the children have not only witnessed the dialogue between the Father and the Son but also understood that the dialogue is intended for them.

Second, there is a transition in the dialogue. The first ten chapters of Hebrews focus on the Father's dialogue with the Son. The last three chapters focus on the Father's dialogue with the children (believers). The Father's first words to the Son are *"You are my Son, today I have begotten you"* (Hebrews 1:5; emphasis added). In His last words in Hebrews, the Father addresses the children with the same expression: *"My son, do not regard lightly the discipline of the Lord"* (Hebrews 12:5; emphasis added). Also, in His first response, the Son says, referring to the Father: "I will put my trust in him" (Hebrews 2:13). At the end of the document, the first and only response of the children to the Father expresses the same trust: "The Lord is my helper; I will not fear" (Hebrews 13:5). What the author is saying is that we need to follow the example of Jesus. There needs to be a transition from the faithfulness of the Son to the faithfulness of the children.

Third, God's words do not simply provide information about the Son or to the Son but are acts *on* or *for* the Son. Thus, in His first speech act, God appoints the Son Ruler over the universe (Hebrews 1:5–14). In His second speech act, God appoints the Son "priest forever, after the order of Melchizedek" (Hebrews 5:5, 6) and inaugurates a new covenant (Hebrews 8:6–12; cf. 7:21, 22). Thus, God has seated Jesus at His right hand as Ruler for the children's benefit. God has appointed Jesus High Priest for their benefit. More importantly, Jesus is the forerunner of the children (Hebrews 6:19, 20). They will receive a kingdom (Hebrews 12:28; cf. 2:5–10), and they are also priests with Him (Hebrews 13:10–16; cf. 10:19–25). God is saying to His children, "Pay attention to what I say and do with Jesus because what I am doing with Him, I will do with you. Where He is, you will be! *Jesus is My message to you.*"

In summary, the epistle describes God as speaking to believers *in* Jesus (Hebrews 1:1, 2; 12:25–29). What has God said? God has installed Jesus as Ruler of the universe (Hebrews 1:5–14), appointed Him High Priest of the heavenly sanctuary (Hebrews 5:5, 6), and made Him Guarantor of the new covenant (Hebrews 7:21, 22). Jesus' exaltation as King, Priest, and Mediator is for the benefit of believers; He is the anchor of their hope (Hebrews 6:19, 20). Therefore, every cycle in the dialogue ends with an extended exhortation to hear the voice of God and take advantage of the opportunities God has provided in Jesus.[5]

---

1. Hebrews 2:1–4; 3:7–11; 4:12, 13; 5:11–14; 12:18–29.

2. Pamela Michelle Eisenbaum, *The Jewish Heroes of Christian History: Hebrews 11 in Literary Context*, Society of Biblical Literature Dissertation Series 156 (Atlanta: Scholars Press, 1997), 92; emphasis in the original; see also Eisenbaum, 89–133. See also Félix H. Cortez, " 'See That You Do Not Refuse the One Who Is Speaking': Hearing God Preach and Obedience in the Letter to the Hebrews," *Journal of the Adventist Theological Society* 19, nos. 1–2 (2008): 98–108.

3. Eisenbaum, *The Jewish Heroes*, 109.

4. These are, in fact, messages of hope for God's people of deliverance from their enemies. Félix H. Cortez, *The Letter to the Hebrews*, Seventh-day Adventist International Bible Commentary (Nampa, ID: Pacific Press®, forthcoming).

5. Hebrews 3:1–4:16 (cf. 2:1–4); 5:11–6:20; 10:19–12:29.

Three

Jesus,
the Promised Son

The most important title of Jesus in Hebrews is not that He is a priest or a ruler, but that He is a "Son"—the "Son of God." Whenever Jesus is compared with institutions or characters of the Old Testament—for example, the angels (Hebrews 1:5–14), Moses (Hebrews 3:1–6), or Aaron (Hebrews 7:26–28)—it is the fact that He is the Son, while they are not, that sets Him apart as superior. Furthermore, Jesus sits at the right hand of God as Ruler and has been appointed as High Priest because He is the Son (Hebrews 1:3–14; 5:5, 6).

This leads to several important questions: What does it mean that Jesus is the Son of God? Why is He not described here as an Associate, a Partner, a Friend, or simply God's fellow Divine Being? If Jesus is the Son of God, how and when was He begotten as the Son? Finally, if Jesus is the Son, what does that mean for us, who are also God's children? Is He the older brother, suggesting that He is one among many? Is Jesus the perfect, favorite son? Or is He *the* Son—that is to say, a different kind of son? To answer these questions, we need to understand what the Bible says about the "son of God."

Adam, son of God

The first person to be called "son of God" in the Bible is Adam: "The son of Enos, the son of Seth, the son of *Adam, the son of God*" (Luke 3:38; emphasis added). Genesis 5:1–3 explains that being created in the image of God implies a father-son relationship: "When God created man [Adam], he made him in the likeness of God. Male and female he created them, and he blessed them and named them Man [Adam] when they were created. When Adam had lived 130 years, *he fathered a son in his own likeness, after his image*, and named him Seth" (emphasis added). Genesis also says that human beings were the only creatures created in the image of God (Genesis 1:26).

I would like to focus on two elements of the image of God.[1] First, the Hebrew words *tselem* ("image," in concrete terms) and *demut* ("likeness," in abstract terms) suggest that human beings resemble God both in their outward, physical form and in their mental and spiritual nature. Ellen G. White concurs: "When Adam came from the Creator's hand, he bore, in his physical, mental, and spiritual nature, a likeness to his Maker."[2] Second, human beings resemble God in authority and status. They are coregents of God. Thus, they have dominion over the earth and should subdue it (Genesis 1:28; Psalm 8:3–8). They are the king and queen of the earthly domain.

Human beings, however, abused their privileges, and the father-son relationship was frayed (Genesis 3). The image of God in human beings was severely damaged, and their physical, mental, spiritual, and relational powers were greatly diminished.[3] Human beings were cast out from their inheritance, and a new ruler obtained dominion over the earth (Genesis 3; John 12:31).[4]

Israel, son of God

The second person to be called "son of God" was Israel: "Then you shall say to Pharaoh, 'Thus says the LORD, *Israel is my firstborn son*, and I say to you, "Let *my son* go that he may serve me." If you refuse to let him go, behold, I will kill your firstborn son'" (Exodus 4:22, 23;

34

emphasis added).[5] The function of Adam was to mediate as coregent the benevolent rule of God over all creation. Now, God wants Israel to fulfill that function so that through them, all the nations or families of the earth will be blessed (Genesis 12:3; 22:18). God had commanded Adam to be fruitful and multiply and fill the earth (Genesis 1:28). Now, He promises to multiply Israel and make it exceedingly fruitful.[6] God had given Adam dominion over the earth. Now, He promises to make the seed of Abraham a great nation (Genesis 12:2). Abraham and his seed would have dominion and be the father of many nations, referring to the fact that they would be the suzerain of many peoples (Genesis 17:4). God also gave them Canaan as an inheritance (Genesis 15:7). Israel was now the son of God, a second Adam.

But Israel was also unfaithful: "But like Adam they transgressed the covenant; there they dealt faithlessly with me" (Hosea 6:7). Thus, God's people were expelled from their inheritance, and their dominion was given to other nations: Babylon, Media-Persia, Greece, and Rome.

The Davidic Messiah, Son of God

The third person to be called "son of God" was the Messiah, the Davidic king promised to Israel: "When your days are fulfilled and you lie down with your fathers, I will raise up your offspring after you, who shall come from your body, and I will establish his kingdom. He shall build a house for my name, and I will establish the throne of his kingdom forever. *I will be to him a father, and he shall be to me a son*" (2 Samuel 7:12–14; emphasis added).

The dominion originally promised to Adam and then to Israel is now given to the promised Davidic king. God Himself will establish His throne:

> "The enemy shall not outwit him;
>   the wicked shall not humble him.
> I will crush his foes before him
>   and strike down those who hate him. . . .

He shall cry to me, 'You are my Father,
   my God, and the Rock of my salvation.'
And *I will make him the firstborn,*
   the highest of the kings of the earth" (Psalm 89:22, 23, 26, 27;
   emphasis added).[7]

Note that just as Yahweh is the "Most High" (*elyon*) God, the Messiah will be the "highest [*elyon*] of the kings of the earth" (verse 27). He will rule in the resemblance of God. He also receives an inheritance. God gives the Messiah the nations as His "heritage" and "the ends of the earth" as His possession (Psalm 2:8). The Messiah is not given to Israel alone but to the world. Thus, when David received the promise, he understood it as an "instruction for mankind" (2 Samuel 7:19).

The Davidic kings, however, transgressed the covenant, and their dominion was taken away. Thus, Ezekiel proclaimed the Lord's decree shortly before the fall of Jerusalem: "Remove the turban and take off the crown. Things shall not remain as they are" (Ezekiel 21:26). On page 179 of *Education*, Ellen G. White further explains: "The crown removed from Israel passed successively to the kingdoms of Babylon, Medo-Persia, Greece, and Rome. God says, 'It shall be no more, until He come whose right it is; and I will give it Him' " (quoting Ezekiel 21:27). Thus, the crown passed from the lineage of David to the lineages of Nebuchadnezzar, Cyrus, Alexander the Great, and Caesar.

The Last Adam

Despite the unfaithfulness of His children, God never gave up on them (2 Timothy 2:13). When the fullness of time came, God sent forth Jesus to redeem humanity.

Jesus defeated the serpent at the cross, which the Bible often calls "the tree."[8] There, where Adam and Eve had attempted to become "like God" (Genesis 3:5), Jesus emptied Himself, took human nature, became a servant, and "humbled himself by becoming obedient to the point of death, even death on a cross" (Philippians 2:5–8). Thus, "the last Adam became a life-giving spirit" (1 Corinthians 15:45; cf. Romans 5:12–21).

Jesus is also the true Seed of Abraham (Galatians 3:16). He came from Egypt (Matthew 2:15), and after crossing the Jordan River, He entered the desert for forty days, where He remained faithful despite Satan's temptations. Jesus is the faithful, obedient Son that we, the seed of Abraham, were not.

Jesus is also the son of David (Matthew 1:1). He is the "righteous Branch" that would be called "the LORD is our righteousness" (Jeremiah 23:5, 6). Jesus is the "righteous one," whom God raised from the dead (Acts 3:14, 15)[9] and seated Him at His right hand (Acts 2:31–35). Thus, Jesus has received all authority in heaven and on Earth (Matthew 28:18), and His rule will never end (Luke 1:31–33). Jesus is the Son of God because He has taken the place of Adam and Israel, as the promised Davidic king or Messiah, to recover what Adam had lost.

"Today, I have begotten you"
When did Jesus become the only "begotten" Son of God? At the Ascension, when He was seated at the right hand of God as the Ruler of the world. That is the witness of Scripture. Thus, Luke reports the words spoken to Mary at the Annunciation: Jesus *will be called* the Son of the Most High. And the Lord God *will give to him the throne* of his father David" (Luke 1:32; emphasis added). Paul explains that Jesus "was declared to be the Son of God in power according to the Spirit of holiness *by his resurrection from the dead*" (Romans 1:4; emphasis added), which was the moment that Jesus was exalted.[10] Jesus became the Son of God when He defeated the usurping ruler of this world and took His seat at God's right hand, recovering what Adam had lost (John 12:31).

The title *Son of God*, however, has gained a depth of meaning with Jesus that it did not have with Adam and Israel. Just as "son of man" means human being (Psalm 8:4), "son of God" may mean divine.[11] Human beings and Israel carried the image of God but were not divine. Jesus, however, is God Himself. He is "the radiance [not reflection] of the glory of God and the exact imprint of his nature" (Hebrews 1:3). Jesus receives worship and is addressed as "O God" because He created the universe (verses 6–12). Jesus is not simply the Inheritor and Ruler of the earth but of "all things"—the universe (verse 2). As John Webster said, "God's speaking ἐν υἱῷ ["in the Son"] is God speaking in person."[12] Thus, "when the fullness of time had come, God sent forth his Son, born of woman, born under the law, to redeem those who were under the law, so that we might receive adoption as sons" (Galatians 4:4, 5). So great is this act of love that the Bible calls it the "mystery of godliness" (1 Timothy 3:16)—a mystery that neither Satan nor we will be able to fathom.[13]

The Son and the children

The title *Son of God* and the name *Adam* have special natures. They identify both a group and a specific person. The person who carries the name *Adam*, then, is both part of the group *and* represents the group. Thus, *Adam* means "humanity" but is also the personal name of the first person created. Note how the name *Adam* functions in the following passage: "This is the book of the generations of *Adam*. When God created *man [Adam]*, he made him in the likeness of God. Male and female he created them, and he blessed them and named them *Man [Adam]* when they were created. When *Adam* had lived 130 years, he fathered a son in his own likeness, after his image, and named him Seth" (Genesis 5:1–3; emphasis added).

Likewise, as Son of God, Jesus both represents humanity and is part of it. Note that Acts 17:28, 29 asserts that we are all sons of God, and the genealogy of Jesus in Luke 3 implies that we are all sons of God. We cannot explore this now, but the important thing is that the benefits that God bestows upon Jesus will be enjoyed by all those who are represented by Him or, in the words of Paul, all those who are "in him" (e.g., Romans 8:1). When God said to Jesus, "You are my beloved Son; with you I am well pleased" (Mark 1:11), He was not speaking to Jesus but to us all. Pay close attention to what Ellen White says about Jesus' prayer at His baptism:

> The Saviour's glance seems to penetrate heaven as He pours out His soul in prayer. . . . *He asks for the witness that God accepts humanity in the person of His Son. . . .*
>
> And the word that was spoken to Jesus at the Jordan, "This is My beloved Son, in whom I am well pleased," *embraces humanity. God spoke to Jesus as our representative.* With all our sins and weaknesses, we are not cast aside as worthless. "He hath made us accepted in the Beloved." Ephesians 1:6. The glory that rested upon Christ is a pledge of the love of God for us. . . . The light which fell from the open portals upon the head of our Saviour will fall upon us as we pray for help to resist temptation. The voice which spoke to Jesus says to every believing soul, This is My beloved child, in whom I am well pleased.[14]

Thus, what God said to Jesus and what God did for Jesus, He also accomplishes for us. God resurrected Jesus, and He will resurrect us too (1 Corinthians 15:20–22). Jesus is seated at God's right hand, and we will enjoy the same privilege (Revelation 3:21). Jesus will judge the world, and we will join Him (1 Corinthians 6:2, 3). "To all who did receive him, who believed in his name, he gave the right to become children of God" (John 1:12).

---

1. For a fuller treatment of the image of God, see Richard M. Davidson, "The Nature of the Human Being From the Beginning: Genesis 1–11," in *"What Are Human Beings That You Remember Them?": Proceedings of the Third International Bible Conference, Nof Ginosar and Jerusalem, June 11–21, 2012,* ed. Clinton Wahlen (Silver Spring, MD: Biblical Research Institute, 2015), 17–22.

2. Ellen G. White, *Education* (Oakland, CA: Pacific Press®, 1903), 15. See also Ellen G. White, *Patriarchs and Prophets* (Battle Creek, MI: Review and Herald®, 1890), 45; Ellen G. White, *The Great Controversy* (Mountain View, CA: Pacific Press®, 1911), 644, 645; Ellen G. White, *Selected Messages,* bk. 3 (Washington, DC: Review and Herald®, 1980), 133.

3. See White, *The Great Controversy*, 644, 645.

4. John 14:30; 16:11; Ephesians 2:2; 6:12.

5. See also Jeremiah 3:19; 31:9, 20; Hosea 11:1.

6. Genesis 12:3; 15:5; 17:6; 22:17, 18; cf. 1:28.

7. See also Psalms 2:8–11; 110:5, 6.

8. Colossians 2:13–15; cf. Acts 5:30; 10:39; 13:29; Galatians 3:13; 1 Peter 2:24.

9. Acts 7:52; 22:14; Romans 1:16, 17; 1 Corinthians 1:30.

10. See also Acts 13:32–39.

11. See also Numbers 23:19; Job 16:21, ESV; Psalm 146:3; Isaiah 51:12; Ezekiel 2:1, etc.

12. John Webster, "One Who Is Son," in *The Epistle to the Hebrews and Christian Theology*, ed. Richard Bauckham, Daniel R. Driver, Trevor A. Hart, and Nathan MacDonald (Grand Rapids, MI: Eerdmans, 2009), 80; see also 78–81.

13. See Ellen G. White, *The Desire of Ages* (Oakland, CA: Pacific Press®, 1898), 115.

14. White, 111–113; emphasis added.

Four

Jesus, Our Faithful Brother

There was a practice in ancient Mesopotamia known as the substitute king ritual, which throws light on what Jesus has done for us.[1] When bad omens that were understood as threatening the king's life occurred, a substitute king was chosen. (For example, these bad omens were an imminent eclipse of the sun, the moon, or one of the planets.) The idea was that the substitute king would attract the effects of the bad omens to his own person and thus protect the king. The substitute was chosen by diviners and was warned that he would take the evil omens upon himself. He was enthroned and dressed like a king, and he received the royal insignias (crown, mantle, weapon, and scepter). He was given a queen who would share his destiny. He played the role of the king by presenting offerings and burning incense but did not rule. He only played the role of the king publicly.

On some occasions, the substitute was a person of high standing. On other occasions, a fool was chosen. (According to Plutarch, the substitute for Alexander the Great was a criminal.)[2] The standing of the individual seemed important, however, because some texts show that simpletons were given high offices before being installed as substitute kings. Once installed, the substitute king took upon himself the threats to the king by reciting the evil omen litanies. Then they were written and folded in the hem of his robe. Finally, at the end of the period, the substitute king and his queen were put to death and given a royal funeral. In this way, the substitute king redeemed the king and the prince, and the land was purified of claims against them so that it could prosper.[3] An ancient text explains this simply and beautifully: "[Damki], the son of the prelate of Akka[d], who had ru[led] Assyria, Babylon(ia) [and] all the countries, [di]ed with his queen on the night o[f the xth day as] a substitute for the king, my lord, [and for the sake of the li]fe of Samas-sumu-uki[n]. He went to his fate for their redemption."[4]

Similarly, Jesus died as the substitute king of Adam and humanity, whom Adam represented, to redeem us from the legal threat of eternal death because of our sins. But the Mesopotamian practice of the substitute king illustrates rather weakly the depth, complexity, and drama involved in our redemption. To begin with, the substitute king is not a fool but God Himself, the Creator and Ruler of the universe. Furthermore, it is true that in some cases, a high official was chosen in ancient Mesopotamia as the substitute king, but the idea was to protect the sovereign. In our case, the Sovereign of the universe died to redeem Adam, the subordinate ruler of this world, and the humanity Adam represented. Finally, Jesus, who is God Himself, died as a substitute king to protect us from our sinful selves, not to shelter us from the threats and wrath of the gods. Nevertheless, to better understand the relationship between Jesus and us, we need to understand Israel's conundrum and God's solution for it.

Israel's conundrum

Israel was the inheritor of great and sweeping promises from God. If Israel faithfully obeyed God, carefully doing all of His commandments, He would place it high above the nations as a kingdom of priests and a holy nation (Deuteronomy 28:1; Exodus 19:5, 6). God would bless its people in the city and in the field with fertility (both at home and in the field), abundance, success in their undertakings, victory at war, dominion over their enemies, and preeminence as the head of the nations (Deuteronomy 28:2–13). In summary, God promised them: "You shall only go up and not down, if you obey the commandments of the Lord your God, which I command you today, being careful to do them, and if you do not turn aside from any of the words that I command you today, to the right hand or to the left" (verses 13, 14).

The problem was that Israel was always inconsistent in its obedience. These promises followed on the heels of the great victories Israel had obtained over Sihon, king of the Amorites, and Og, king of Bashan (Numbers 21). But also, right after the spiritual defeats in the desert, the people of Israel complained and were bitten by "fiery serpents" (Numbers 21:6), and more devastatingly in Shittim, they worshiped Baal Peor and committed harlotry with Moabite women (Numbers 25). A few weeks after receiving the amazing promises of the covenant, Israel conquered Jericho. But Achan broke the covenant by stealing some of the treasures of Jericho—treasures that belonged to God and had been devoted to destruction. The result was that Israel's forces were painfully routed in their subsequent war against the small city of Ai. God explained to Joshua, "The people of Israel cannot stand before their enemies" while they allow the transgression of the covenant in their midst (Joshua 7:12).

The people of Israel inherited great and sweeping promises, but those promises hinged on their faithfulness to the laws and requirements of the covenant. And this was their conundrum. They were never able to be fully faithful to God as a nation, so His promises were only partially fulfilled, never reaching complete fruition. God, however, did not give up. Through the Davidic covenant, He established a way of escape from their predicament.

The Davidic covenant

God promised David that He would build a "house" for David—that is, a ruling dynasty. God would raise a "son" for David, whom God would adopt as His own "son," and establish his throne and kingdom forever. That son would build a house for God so that God would dwell in Israel's midst (2 Samuel 7:12–14).

The promises made to David changed the covenantal relationship between God and Israel. An analysis of those promises shows that the promised son came to embody the covenant relationship between God and the nation. Thus, God designated the Davidic heir His "son" and "firstborn,"[5] embodying Israel, who was also called "son" and "first-born."[6] Moreover, God confirmed to him the promises previously given Israel of a "place" where its people would "rest" from their enemies[7] and His permanent presence among them by accepting a "house" to be built for His "name."[8] In other words, God announced that the son promised to David, the Messiah, would be Israel's proxy.[9]

The relationship between the promised son and Israel is fascinating. The son does not replace Israel as the "son of God" but represents it. Similarly, the Davidic covenant does not replace God's covenant with Israel. The laws promulgated at Sinai would continue to apply. In fact, the promised son would build a "house" for the "ark of God" (2 Samuel 7:1, 2) that enshrined the laws given at Sinai (1 Kings 8:9; 2 Chronicles 5:10). Thus, the king and the people would continue to be bound by the commandments proclaimed at Sinai.[10] What really happened is that God's covenant with David engrafted the monarchy into the existing covenantal relationship between God and Israel.

The implications of the Davidic covenant are breathtaking. God's promises to Israel required that all Israel be faithful in order for them to be fulfilled. (Remember what happened with Achan in Joshua 7.)[11] But God's promise to David secured the fulfillment of God's covenantal promises to Israel through the faithfulness of one person—the promised king. The connection between the faithfulness of the king and the fulfillment of God's covenant with the nation is particularly evident in God's confirmation to Solomon of the promises He had made to his father David: "Concerning this house that you are building, *if you* [singular] will walk in my statutes, obey my ordinances, and keep all my commandments by walking in them, then I will establish my promise *with you* [singular], which I made to your father David. I will dwell among the children of Israel, and *will not forsake my people Israel*" (1 Kings 6:12, 13, NRSV; emphasis added). God explicitly informed Solomon that if he was faithful, God's covenantal relationship with the nation would remain. Avraham Gileadi's conclusion is apt: "The Davidic covenant did away with the necessity that all Israel—to a man—maintain loyalty to YHWH in order to merit his protection."[12]

Another astounding aspect is that the Davidic covenant is unconditional. Neither Israel nor David could do anything to break it (2 Samuel 7:12–16).[13] David's sons throughout the generations would rebel against God and break His commandments, and though God would punish them, their unfaithfulness could not revoke His promises. God would remain faithful forever.

The enduring nature of the promise is astonishing. This was possible only because God knew that He was going to send His own Son, born in the house of David. He would live a life of perfect faithfulness to God so that God's promises to Israel would be fulfilled.[14] The Promised Son, God in the flesh, would build in His own body a temple so that God could dwell in our midst and we could see His glory (John 1:14; 2:18–21). Thus, God's promise of a Son to David both confirmed the covenant and transformed it. It transformed a covenant that was conditional on the faithfulness of Israel for the fulfillment of its promises into an unconditional covenant dependent on the faithfulness of God. The Son, by becoming our Representative, mediated a better covenant based upon better promises.[15]

Oh, the depth of the riches and wisdom and knowledge of God! How unsearchable are his judgments and how inscrutable his ways!

"For who has known the mind of the Lord,
 or who has been his counselor?"

45

"Or who has given a gift to him
  that he might be repaid?"

For from him and through him and to him are all things. To
him be glory forever. Amen (Romans 11:33–36).

The faithfulness of the Son

By embodying God's people and being perfectly faithful, Jesus, the
Son, reclaimed and received the inheritance Israel had forfeited.[16] Jesus
truly became the "sure and steadfast anchor of the soul" for the children (Hebrews 6:19). By becoming their substitute, Jesus made available to them all the benefits of His faithfulness and His rights as heir
of the Father.[17]

Jesus' faithfulness is important because it has made possible what
God always had in mind but could not fulfill because of our sinfulness:
fulfilling the covenant promises for us. Thus, by living a perfect life,
Jesus has become the Ruler of the world, recovering what Adam had
lost (Psalm 8:4–8; Matthew 28:18–20). He has direct access to God,
overcoming the separation that was created by the Fall.[18] He has
become "the heir of all things" (Hebrews 1:2). Therefore, the covenant
and purposes of God have been fulfilled in the person of Jesus, our
Faithful Brother.

It is important to note that the benefits Jesus enjoys are not His by
the grace of God but as a fulfillment of a legal covenant promise. God
had bound Himself by an oath that He would bestow all the covenant
blessings upon His obedient children (Exodus 19–24; Deuteronomy
28; 29). Jesus fulfilled the conditions; therefore, the blessings are His.
Amazingly, grace resides in the fact that God sent His Son *as our
Representative* to suffer the covenant curses in our place so that the
covenant blessings could be ours. This is possible because the Son
offered Himself, before the foundation of the world, as a sacrifice to
redeem us.[19] The purpose was that through Him, we all could become
God's children and heirs again![20]

The success of God's purposes was never in doubt because it was never contingent on human faithfulness but on God's own faithfulness (2 Timothy 2:13). What remains in doubt is whether you and I will embrace Jesus' victory and God's saving purposes on our behalf. Israel's conundrum is the same conundrum you and I face: the covenant blessings require perfect obedience. It is, in fact, the same conundrum Adam and Abraham faced. But God, from the very beginning, provided the answer: I will give you a Son, Jesus (Genesis 3:15; 22:18; Galatians 3:16). Those who are "in him"—that is, those who embrace Him, His leadership, and His action in their lives—have fulfilled perfectly the conditions: we will "be found in him, not having a righteousness of . . . [our] own that comes from the law, but that which comes through faith in Christ, the righteousness from God that depends on faith" (Philippians 3:9). "There is therefore now no condemnation for those who are in Christ Jesus" (Romans 8:1).

We are astonishingly slow to understand the magnitude of God's salvation in Jesus. When Jesus approaches the Father to ask the covenant promises on our behalf, He is not asking for a favor. He is demanding the rightful, legal benefits of His faithful life from a Father who set up the system and protected it resolutely so that the Son could make claims in our favor. "Let us then with confidence draw near to the throne of grace, that we may receive mercy and find grace to help in time of need" (Hebrews 4:16).

---

1. See John H. Walton, "The Imagery of the Substitute King Ritual in Isaiah's Fourth Servant Song," *Journal of Biblical Literature* 122, no. 4 (Winter 2003): 734–743, https://doi.org/10.2307/3268075.

2. Walton, 737.

3. Walton, 736–738.

4. Walton, 738.

5. 2 Samuel 7:14; Psalms 2:6, 7; 89:27.

6. Exodus 4:22, 23.

7. 2 Samuel 7:9–11a.

8. 2 Samuel 7:12–16; Psalm 132:11–14.

9. For a full discussion, see Félix H. Cortez, "The Son as the Representative of the Children in the Letter to the Hebrews," in *Son, Sacrifice, and Great Shepherd: Studies on the Epistle to the Hebrews*, ed. David Moffitt and Eric F. Mason, *Wissenschaftliche Untersuchungen zum Neuen Testament* 2, no. 510 (Tübingen, Germany: Mohr Siebeck, 2020), 34, 35.

10. E.g., 1 Kings 6:12, 13.

11. See also Joshua 22:10–34, esp. verse 18, and Numbers 25.

12. Avraham Gileadi, "The Davidic Covenant: A Theological Basis for Corporate Protection," in *Israel's Apostasy and Restoration: Essays in Honor of Roland K. Harrison*, ed. A. Gileadi (Grand Rapids, MI: Baker, 1988), 160.

13. See Cortez, "The Son as the Representative," 37–39.

14. Galatians 4:4–8; Romans 1:3, 4; Luke 1:31–33.

15. Hebrews 8:6.

16. Hebrews 1:2; 2:6–9; 9:15; cf. 4:14–16; 6:19, 20; 9:11–14.

17. See Cortez, "The Son as the Representative," 41.

18. Genesis 3:24; Matthew 27:51; Mark 1:10; Hebrews 10:19–22.

19. John 17:24; Ephesians 1:4; 1 Peter 1:20.

20. John 1:12; Galatians 4:4–7.

Five

Jesus,
the Giver of Rest

In the final years of the 1990s, my parents made a trip to Israel and returned with gifts for us. The gift I remember most was for my son. It was a beautiful sling and a shepherd's pouch, both made of leather. Inside, my mother placed five stones she had picked up from the brook in the Valley of Elah, between ancient Socoh and Azekah, where the famous battle between David and Goliath took place around three thousand years earlier (1 Samuel 17:1–3, 40).

This gift was special for several reasons. First, while it is possible to purchase a sling and a shepherd's pouch in other places, the stones, utterly common and ordinary, were a visual, tangible representation of the land they had just visited. They were more than a representation; they were a piece of that land. Second, my mother explained to the little four-year-old boy that she wanted him to grow up to be strong and brave like the shepherd boy whose story he already knew by heart. The gift was a token of my mother's hopes for her eldest grandson. And third, it was a gift my son could play with. At the time, I was the youth director for the Central Mexican Conference in Mexico City, and I would often ask my son to wear the leather pouch and the sling as an illustration for the sermon I would preach. He enjoyed playing the part of young David and the attention he received. But even more, he enjoyed playing with his gifts. We let him play with the sling but confiscated the stones, worried that he might enthusiastically smash some "Goliaths" around the house or harm the apartment complex where we lived.

The Sabbath as a token of salvation

Like the gifted sling, the Sabbath is about a special relationship. The Bible says that God established the Sabbath as a sign of the covenantal relationship between Him and the people of Israel.[1] The Hebrew word *oth*, translated as "sign" in our Bibles, is very significant. An *oth*, or sign, "is an object, an occurrence, an event through which a person is to *recognize, learn, remember, or perceive* the credibility of something."[2] Signs primarily serve an epistemic function. They *impart knowledge*. They serve as concrete evidence of the truth and reliability of God and of the assertions and promises He has made.

Signs fulfill several functions in the relationship between God and His people. In most cases, they are intended to impart knowledge about the credibility of God. For example, God used the plagues as signs to let Pharaoh and the Egyptians know that His demand that they liberate the children of Israel was backed by His unrivaled power and His supreme authority as Ruler over all the nations and their gods (e.g., Exodus 8:22; 12:12). They were also intended as signs to remind the Israelites "that the LORD is God; there is no other besides him" (Deuteronomy 4:35). Through the miraculous plagues, then, both the Egyptians and the Israelites *knew* that Yahweh is above everything and everyone because they *experienced* His matchless power.

The experiential knowledge a sign provides has legal consequences because it cannot be denied. Thus, when God swore through Jeremiah that He would punish the Israelites who had returned to Egypt, He gave them a sign (*oth*). He told them that when Pharaoh Hophra, king of Egypt, was given into the hands of his enemies, the Israelites who had put their trust in him would *know* that their catastrophe had been sealed (Jeremiah 44:26–30). In this case, the sign served to the Israelites was a concrete, historical event that functioned as a legal, undeniable notification that their fate had been set.

Signs also have other functions. *Signs may protect* because they provide a concrete identification of those whose lives are protected by God. Thus, Cain received a sign that warned other people against killing him (Genesis 4:15), and the blood of the Passover lamb on the doorposts and the lintel protected the life of the firstborn from the destroyer (Exodus 12:13). *Signs may serve a mnemonic function* to keep important truths in mind. Thus, God explained to the people of Israel that the Passover and the unleavened bread feasts were to serve as "a sign" on their hands and as "a memorial" between their eyes that the Lord had set them free from Egypt with a strong hand (Exodus 13:9; see also Joshua 4). God often gave *signs to promote faith and confidence* in Him (e.g., Isaiah 7:1–11). Similarly, prophets sometimes performed peculiar, *symbolic acts that functioned as signs of events* that would happen in the future.[3] Finally, covenants also had visual, concrete marks *to identify those who were part of a covenant.* For example, circumcision served as an external mark of the covenant between God and Abraham (Genesis 17), and likewise, Sabbath observance is an external sign of the relationship between God and His people (Exodus 31:13, 17; Ezekiel 20:12, 20).

Rest and the Sabbath in Hebrews

In the argument of Hebrews, Sabbath observance functions as a sign, or token, of the promise of rest God gave to His people. In Hebrews 3 and 4, it is asserted that Psalm 95 contains a standing invitation to enter into the rest of God. In the Old Testament, the concept of rest refers to the Sabbath God observed at the end of Creation; to the land He gave His people as an inheritance, setting them free from the threat of enemies; or to the temple where God rested.[4] These three elements are intimately connected in Hebrews 3 and 4 and in the rest of the letter. Hebrews 4:3–5 explains that the rest God is inviting us to enter is the rest God entered into at the Sabbath of Creation and has been available for us since then. Hebrews 4:8 compares that rest to the rest God promised Israel in the land of Canaan—a rest that Joshua could not provide. Finally, the invitation to enter rest in Hebrews 4 culminates with the encouragement to draw near with confidence to the throne of grace in the heavenly sanctuary (verses 14–16).

Something similar happens in the macrostructure of the letter to the Hebrews. Hebrews 4 exhorts us to enter into the Sabbath rest God made available to us through Jesus (verses 9–11). Hebrews 5–10 invites us to approach God with confidence through the veil in the heavenly sanctuary because the blood of Jesus has purified our consciences from sin (Hebrews 10:19–23). Finally, Hebrews 10–13 invites us to run with perseverance the race set before us so that we may enter the heavenly homeland—the promised inheritance (Hebrews 11:10–16, 39, 40).

Note, however, that the Promised Land, the temple, and the Sabbath are not, in and of themselves, the rest. They are the geographical and temporal structures that made the rest available. Rest is something that happens within those temporal and geographical structures. This explains why Hebrews 4:8 says that Joshua did not give Israel the rest that God had promised.

It is true that Joshua led the people into the Promised Land and obtained dominion over it.[5] But possession of the land was not the same as rest. Deuteronomy 12:1–14 states that to enter the rest, God wanted the people to possess *all* the land, "from the wilderness to the Lebanon and from the River, the river Euphrates, to the western sea."[6] In addition, He instructed them to *cleanse* the land from idolatry and worship Him in the place He would choose for His name to dwell. But Israel did not conquer all the land in the time of Joshua nor cleanse it from idolatry.

The land, the cleansing, and the place for God's dwelling were the conditions necessary for God to have an intimate, close relationship with His people. God's plan was to bring the Israelites to Himself and live in their midst (Exodus 19:4; 25:8). The land and the temple were the geographical and physical structures that would make an intimate relationship with God possible. The same is true of the Sabbath. Abstention from work on the Sabbath facilitates an intimate relationship with God. Abstention from work, however, is not the same as the rest God has in mind; it only makes it possible. Therefore, the rest in Hebrews refers to the new covenant benefit of confident, intimate access to God Himself (Hebrews 10:19–23). This benefit has been made available to us through the blood of Jesus Christ. It implies the restoration of the Edenic ideal of a confident, intimate relationship with God that existed on the Sabbath of Creation.

Sabbath observance as a token of God's rest

Hebrews refers to the rest God invites us to enter as a Sabbath rest (Hebrews 4:9) because the Sabbath rest functions as the sign of the new covenant promise of confident intimacy with Him. In fact, it embodies, or epitomizes, that promise. The Sabbath as a covenant sign involves the following elements:

1. The Sabbath has the function of communicating knowledge. When God gave the Sabbath to His people as the sign of their covenant relationship, He explained its purpose in the following way: "*That you may know* that I, the LORD, sanctify you" (Exodus 31:13; emphasis added). Sabbath observance provides the *experiential* knowledge that through our sanctification, we have been separated from other nations. The intimacy we experience with God on the Sabbath reveals to us that we are special. This knowledge cannot be transferred to others. It has to be experienced personally. Without intimacy, there is no revelation; there is no knowledge. Intimacy with God in the Sabbath is a foretaste, a token, of the kind of intimacy we will experience with God in heaven throughout eternity. This foretaste of the future intimacy provides an assurance of our future redemption.

2. The Sabbath has a protective function. It is a visual, concrete identification of the people of God who recognize Him as the Creator of all things and, therefore, the Ruler and Judge of all things (Revelation 14:6, 7). That identification makes possible God's protection (Revelation 7:1–3).

3. Sabbath observance has a mnemonic function that promotes faith. It reminds believers that God created all things and has the power to provide for all their needs (Exodus 20:8–11). It also reminds them that God redeemed them and that He can provide for all their spiritual needs (Deuteronomy 5:12–15). Communally, the Sabbath allows believers to meet together to exhort and encourage one another to faith and good works (Hebrews 3:12, 13; 10:23–25). Sabbath observance protects God's people against the forgetfulness that leads to apostasy.

4. Sabbath observance is a symbolic act. It is the external, concrete manifestation of an internal reality. We prepare by cleaning our homes because we have also cleansed the temple of the soul, preparing for God's visit. We stop working because we recognize that we are saved by grace through faith. Sabbath is an affirmation that our faith is not in our job, our social or family relationships, or even our efforts and abilities. Sabbath observance says that our faith is put in God and He takes priority. We worship on Sabbath because no other day memorializes God as our Creator and Redeemer. We wear our best clothes and eat the choicest meals because Sabbath is a day of celebration—a foretaste of the moment we will enjoy the supper of the Lamb and put on the immortal glorious body. When we keep the Sabbath, we say something to God and to others. We say that we are in a covenant relationship with Him. No other religious act can express the depth and breadth of that commitment.

The Sabbath rest functions similarly to the gift my mother brought my son from the Holy Land. It is a little piece of heaven that we can enjoy here and now. The Sabbath communicates God's deepest desires for us, and when we observe the Sabbath, we communicate our joyful acceptance of His promises.

Let us therefore strive to enter that rest

It is important to note that Hebrews 3 and 4 are not an invitation to rest but a plea to *enter* that rest (Hebrews 4:11). Jesus explained in Matthew 11:28–30 *how* we can enter the rest. We need to take His yoke and work with Him. Jesus is also inviting us to follow His example and enjoy personal intimacy with Him. He is the One who gives rest. He explained what God had said to Moses: "My presence will go with you, and I will give you rest" (Exodus 33:14).

Many years ago, a friend invited me to play frontenis (similar to racquetball) with him on the public courts on a Sunday morning. At first, I hesitated to accept the invitation because I barely knew how to play the game. He assured me that my inexperience would not be a factor because he would join me on a doubles team. He had been a professional athlete at the national level and was an excellent player. When we arrived at the court, I felt intimidated by the other team's high level of play, but he told me, "Don't worry, just serve the ball, and I will do the rest." And that is what he did. I served the ball throughout the game, and he dealt with the difficult shots that came at us in response to my weak, easy serves. He was spectacular, returning their difficult shots and even some that I thought were unanswerable. We did not lose a game.

Today Jesus invites you to join His team. He is the ultimate doubles Partner. For those who accept the invitation to wear His yoke, the crushing burdens of life are lifted, and the journey becomes easy, light, and joyful.

---

1. Exodus 31:13, 17; Ezekiel 20:12, 20.

2. F. H. Helfmeyer, "אוֹת," in *Theological Dictionary of the Old Testament*, ed. G. Johannes Botterweck and Helmer Ringgren, trans. John T. Willis et al. (Grand Rapids, MI: Eerdmans, 1974), 1:170; emphasis added.

3. E.g., Isaiah 20; Ezekiel 4.

4. Sabbath: Exodus 35:2; Genesis 2:2; Exodus 20:11; Deuteronomy 5:12–15. Land: Deuteronomy 12:10; Exodus 33:14; Deuteronomy 25:19; Joshua 1:13, 15; 21:44; 22:4; 23:1. Sanctuary: 1 Kings 8:56; 2 Chronicles 6:41; Psalm 132:8, 13, 14; Isaiah 66:1.

5. Deuteronomy 25:19; Joshua 1:13, 15; 21:44; 22:4.

6. Deuteronomy 11:24. This is the land God had promised Abraham and confirmed to Moses: Genesis 15:18; Exodus 23:31; Numbers 34:1–15; Deuteronomy 1:7, 8.

Six

Jesus,
the Faithful Priest

A *priest* is a person who mediates between God and man. The Latin word for priest, *pontifex*, means "bridge maker." It focuses on the priest's function, which is to bridge the divide between the human and the divine realms. The Greek word for priest, *hiereus*, belongs to a group of words related to *hieros*, which means "mighty or holy."[1] It focuses on the main characteristic of a priest—his holiness—which allows the priest to have access to the divine realm. Thus, since the function of a priest is to mediate between frail human beings and a powerful and holy God, the priest's most important ability is to have *access* to both parties and represent them well. A successful priest, then, must be able to faithfully represent the people to whom he or she belongs and have true access to God and accurately represent His instructions and will.

According to the Old Testament, the mediating role of the priests involved several important functions. Some of them were related to their role as representatives of God before the people, and other functions were related to their role as representatives of the people before God.

The priest as representative of the people

The most obvious function of the priests was their role of representing the people before God. The high priest embodied God's ideals for the nation in his person; the special clothing he wore symbolized this. The dress of the priest was white, made of fine linen, and had five different elements: (1) breeches, or shorts, that went from the waist to the knees and functioned as "undergarments to cover their naked flesh" (Exodus 28:42); (2) a tunic with sleeves, "woven in one piece,"[2] that went from the shoulders to the feet (Exodus 39:27); (3) a white linen miter as headdress (Exodus 28:40); (4) an embroidered or checkered robe (verse 39) that went over the tunic; and (5) a white linen girdle that held the robe, embroidered in blue, purple, and red (Exodus 28:39; 39:29). This dress had an important symbolic function. The white linen material and the detailed embroidery represented the purity and beauty of character that God expected from His ministers and His people. Thus, the prophet John explained later that the white linen represented "the righteous acts of the saints" (Revelation 19:8, NASB; cf. 15:6).

The attire of the high priest was even more impressive. It was "for glory and for beauty" (Exodus 28:2). It added five pieces to the dress already mentioned for the priests. These were golden, multicolored pieces. First, there was a blue woolen cloak that reached from the shoulders to just below the knees. All around the hem of this cloak were attached blue, purple, and scarlet pomegranates and golden bells (verses 31–35).

Second, there was a sleeveless, two-piece ephod made with the same materials that the veil was made out of—blue, purple, and scarlet thread. This ephod was connected on the shoulders with two onyx stones upon which were carved the names of the twelve tribes of Israel—six on each stone. These were "stones of remembrance for the sons of Israel" so that Aaron would "bear their names before the Lord" (verse 12).

Third, a sash made with the same materials as the ephod (verses 8,

27, 28). Fourth, the "breastplate of judgment," also made of the same material as the ephod (verse 15). It contained twelve jewels, and in each of them was engraved the name of one of the tribes of Israel. In addition, the breastplate of judgment also contained the Urim and Thummim, stones through which God answered specific questions asked by His people. The purpose of the breastplate was that the high priest would "bear the names of the sons of Israel in the breastpiece of judgment on his heart, when he goes into the Holy Place, to bring them to regular remembrance before the LORD" (verse 29). The breastplate provided a visual and symbolic identification of the high priest as the representative of the people.

Finally, there was a turban with a golden plate with the inscription "Holy to the LORD," which identified the high priest as the ruler of his people (verses 36, 37). God Himself designed every aspect of the priestly garments. The beauty and splendor of the priestly attire expressed the lofty plans God had for His people. Israel was God's treasured possession—a kingdom of priests and a holy nation (Exodus 19:5, 6).

The high priest represented and embodied the nation of Israel. As the representative of the people, the priest presented on behalf of the Israelites all the gifts and sacrifices they brought to God because the Israelites themselves could not approach God in the sanctuary (Numbers 1:50–53; cf. Exodus 33:20).

The priest also represented Israel in a more critical way. When an Israelite brought a sacrifice to expiate for his or her sin, the priest ate part of the sacrifice so that he "may bear the iniquity of the congregation" (Leviticus 10:17). To "bear the iniquity" means liability to punishment (Leviticus 5:1). In other words, a person who sinned was liable to punishment by God, but when he or she repented and brought a sacrifice for expiation, a sin offering, liability for that punishment was transferred to the priest, who "bore" it—that is, assumed it. Of course, the priest could not suffer the punishment for all the sins of Israel, but he was a type of Jesus, the true Priest and Representative of Israel who would come and bear our sins on the cross (Isaiah 54:5; Colossians 2:14).

The priest as a representative of God

The priest also represented God before the people. The performance of this function was crucial for the relationship between God and His people. The duties of the priest as a representative of God can be organized into five categories.

First, priests were agents for God. They protected the sacred things and the sacred space from encroachment by non-Levites (Numbers 3:10; 18:1–7). They also purified and consecrated objects and persons so that they could be used for holy purposes or the service of God (Leviticus 4–6; 12; 15; 16).

Second, the priest was a teacher of the law (Leviticus 10:11).[3] He explained to the people the rules and meaning of the cult, the story of God's care for Israel, and His grace. This implied reading; narration; explanation; translation, if necessary (Nehemiah 8:8); and copying and preserving the writings with God's instructions (Ezra 7:6). The prophet Malachi explained God's expectations: "For the lips of a priest should guard knowledge, and people should seek instruction from his mouth, for he is the messenger of the LORD of hosts" (Malachi 2:7).

Third, priests had the important function of interpreting and applying God's laws and principles to specific situations. They were to make God's abstract principles and rules into concrete and understandable actions and practices. For example, they were to explain and apply purity laws, tithes, offerings, and other contributions when Israelites were in doubt or unsure.[4]

Fourth, priests were judges. They assisted the judges of every town in difficult matters, and the high priest functioned as the nation's chief justice.[5]

And last, priests were spokesmen for God. For example, the priests were entrusted with invoking the blessing of God upon the people of Israel.[6] Their role was to put the name of God upon Israel so that God would bless them. This implies a great privilege and a great power. This is what God envisioned His people as a nation would do for all the world (Genesis 12:1–3). The high priest also carried the Urim and Thummim, two stones through which God revealed His will regarding specific questions asked by the people.[7]

The failure of the priesthood

The priests, however, were never able to completely fulfill God's purpose for them. The high and lows of the priesthood throughout Israel's history were both a factor in and a reflection of the spiritual condition of the people. Nadab and Abihu, the children of the first high priest, perished because they offered "unauthorized fire before the Lord" (Leviticus 10:1). Centuries later, the iniquity and negligence of the priests led to the fall of Israel and Judah. The priests had not simply been derelict in their duty to teach the law but led immoral lives and misled the people.[8] After the Exile, their ministry did not improve, and God warned that He would expel them from the ministry, together with their disrespectful sacrifices and service.[9]

The priesthood, however, reached its nadir in the time of Jesus, which was one of the factors that led to the fall of Jerusalem. The office of the priesthood was controlled by the Romans, who sold it to the highest bidder (b. Yoma 18a). As a result, of the twenty-eight high priests who held the high priestly office between 37 BC and the fall of Jerusalem in AD 70, only the first and the last belonged to a legitimate family. Four wealthy illegitimate families controlled the priesthood during that time: the families of Boethus, Annas, Phiabi, and Kamith.[10] Their power came from their money, nepotism, and ruthlessness.[11] The Talmud, for example, has complaints about the violence of the high priests who forcibly appropriated the hides of the sacrifices that should have been distributed among all the officiant priests.[12] Josephus also reports that the chief priests sent their servants to threshing floors to violently seize the tithes, thus robbing sustenance from the poorer priests.[13]

The faithful priest

The book of Hebrews tells us, however, that God set aside the Levitical priesthood because of its weakness and uselessness, which was a kind way to refer to the failure and wickedness of the Jewish priestly aristocracy of the time, and appointed a faithful Priest over the house of God (Hebrews 7:11–19; 3:1–6).

Jesus fulfilled all the purposes God had envisioned for the priesthood. He is the perfect Agent through which God cleansed, consecrated, and saved us. Jesus died on the cross as a sacrifice to cleanse us from our sins (Hebrews 9:14–17; 10:10–14). Jesus defeated the devil in His life and at the cross to deliver us from Satan's power (Hebrews 2:14–16), and He will bring us to glory (Hebrews 2:10; 12:28). Jesus is the perfect Teacher, who writes the law of God in our hearts and on our minds (Hebrews 8:10). As Judge, He will vindicate us in the final judgment and will come to deliver us (Hebrews 9:27, 28). Jesus is also the perfect Spokesman who not only speaks the word of God but is the Word of God Himself, embodying the perfect fulfillment of God's instructions, laws, and dreams for us. His resurrection and exaltation demonstrate the rewards for a life of obedience and faithfulness to God (Hebrews 1:1, 2; 12:1–4; cf. Matthew 5:17–20).

More importantly, however, He is our perfect Representative because He is one of us. He became flesh and blood, suffered temptation, and experienced rejection and shame, just as we have. He also triumphed, just as we will (Hebrews 2:5–9, 14–18; 4:15, 16; 5:7–9; 7:26–28). He bore our sins and suffered the penalty for them that we might live the benefits of His perfect life of obedience (Hebrews 9:28; cf. verses 15–22). Therefore, He has restored our relationship with God and provided us with full and confident access to His presence (Hebrews 4:15, 16; 10:19–22). His presence at the right hand of God guarantees that all these benefits are available to us (Hebrews 6:19, 20; 7:22; 8:6).

We are His house: The priesthood of all believers

Hebrews also teaches us that we are of the house of Jesus, the High

Priest (Hebrews 3:6), which means that we are all priests (Hebrews 10:19–21; cf. 1 Peter 2:5, 9). We were washed with water and cleansed through the sprinkling of blood by Jesus' sacrifice, just as Aaron and his children were consecrated to the priesthood (Hebrews 10:19–22; cf. Exodus 29; Leviticus 8). We serve as agents of God under the leadership of Jesus for the benefit of our fellow human beings. We carry God's name and represent in our lives the principles of His kingdom (Hebrews 6:10; 13:15). We were sanctified to approach God confidently in the sanctuary to find grace and help, not only for us but also for others (Hebrews 4:16). We serve Him by offering sacrifices of praise, good works, and sharing what we have and thus become blessings to all human beings (Hebrews 13:15, 16). "May the God of peace who brought again from the dead our Lord Jesus" equip us "with everything good" that we may do His will, "working in us that which is pleasing in his sight, through Jesus Christ" (verses 20, 21).

---

1. Edward Ross Wharton, *Etyma Graeca: An Etymological Lexicon of Classical Greek* (London: Percival, 1890), 60.

2. Ellen G. White, *Patriarchs and Prophets* (Battle Creek, MI: Review and Herald®, 1890), 350.

3. Deuteronomy 31:9–13 explains that at least once every seven years, the law should be read to all the people.

4. E.g., Leviticus 10:10, 11; Exodus 23:19; Leviticus 27:1–33.

5. Deuteronomy 17:8–13; 19:16, 17; 21:1–5.

6. Numbers 6:22–27; cf. Deuteronomy 10:8; Leviticus 9:22.

7. Ellen G. White explains how this happened: "When questions were brought for decision before the Lord, a halo of light encircling the precious stone at the right [Urim] was a token of the divine consent or approval, while a cloud shadowing the stone at the left [Thummim] was an evidence of denial or disapprobation." *Patriarchs and Prophets*, 351.

8. Hosea 4:4–14; Micah 3:11; Ezekiel 22:26. See also Jeremiah 2:8; 5:31; 6:13; 8:8–10; 14:18; 18:18; 23:33; 32:32; Lamentations 4:13; Malachi 2:1–9.

9. Malachi 1:6–2:9; cf. Nehemiah 13:4–14.

10. Joachim Jeremias, *Jerusalem in the Time of Jesus* (Philadelphia: Fortress, 1962), 194. For a list of high priests, see 377, 378.

11. Jeremias, 195, 196. See also Acts 4.5, 6.

12. E.g., b. Pesah. 57a. See Jeremias, 180, 181.

13. Josephus, *Jewish Antiquities* 20.181, 206.

Seven

Jesus,
the Anchor of the Soul

How is it possible that the readers of Hebrews, who had been willing to lose their possessions and suffer public shame for Christ, were now in danger of falling away from Him, even to the point of crucifying Him? (Hebrews 6:4–6; cf. 10:32–34). How does a person go from resolute faithfulness to abandoning the path and even joining those who despise Jesus? The answers to these questions center on our assurance in Christ—a topic that is the central concern of Hebrews 6. What, then, is assurance in Christ? How can it be obtained?

The danger of apostasy
The apostle Paul explains that the problem with his readers was that they had stopped growing (Hebrews 5:11–14). They had contented themselves with the basic stuff, the elementary doctrine of Christ, and had not expanded their knowledge with more advanced understanding.

The apostle points out, for example, that they were having trouble understanding the priestly sacrifice and ministry in their favor, which he had just mentioned in Hebrews 5:1–10. This is why they continued to offer sacrifices in the temple and to seek the Levitical priestly mediation. The author warns them that if they continue on that path, they will eventually apostatize from Christ and crucify Him again (Hebrews 6:4–6). Those strong words probably startled the audience.

The warning of the apostle raises some important questions for us. Is salvation dependent on theological understanding? Does deeper theological understanding improve, or even ensure, our chances of remaining faithful to Jesus? Does difficulty in understanding increase the chances of apostasy?

The key to assurance of salvation is not theological understanding itself. The Bible has many examples of individuals, from Lucifer to Judas, who apostatized in spite of a deep understanding of God and Jesus. The basis for assurance lies elsewhere. When we discern why a person is able to grow in knowledge while others are not, we will understand what the relationship between knowledge and assurance is. Let me explain with a story that happened several years ago.[1]

In September 1983, Gianfranco Becchina, an Italian art dealer, communicated with the J. Paul Getty Museum that he had a magnificent marble statue, made in the sixth century BC. The statue was a kouros—a representation of a naked young man, common in the ancient Greek world. Becchina asked for $10 million.

The museum analyzed the offer with caution. It took the kouros on loan to do an in-depth investigation, which lasted fourteen months. The Getty Museum concluded that the style of the sculpture was similar to the Anavyssos kouros at the National Archaeological Museum of Greece in Athens. The Getty's attorneys concluded that the documents certifying the recent history of the statue were genuine.

The Getty Museum also contracted the services of Stanley Margolis, a geologist from the University of California, Davis. Margolis dedicated two days to examining the surface of the statue with a stereo high-definition microscope. Then he took a sample and examined it with an electron microscope; he performed mass spectrometry, x-ray diffraction, and x-ray fluorescence. In his report, Margolis observed that the material was dolomite from the ancient quarry at Vathi on the island of Thassos and that the surface was covered with a thin layer of calcite. Margolis explained that dolomite could transform itself into calcite only through a process that lasts hundreds or thousands of years, which demonstrated that the statue could not be a recent falsification. The Getty Museum purchased the statue for $9 million.

The story is extraordinary because when the kouros was first put on exhibition, many ancient art experts immediately concluded that it was a fake. They had excavated and personally studied many ancient statues and knew that this particular one could not be genuine.

Eight years later, on May 25–27, 1992, scholars devoted an entire congress to discussing the kouros of the Getty Museum. As a result, the formidable scientific argument for the authenticity of the kouros begun to crumble. A zip code mentioned in the original documents of the kouros did not exist until twenty years after the date of the documents. A bank account mentioned in them had also been opened eight years later. The style of the kouros was, in fact, a pastiche of different styles from several periods and several places. A geologist also demonstrated that the thin layer of calcite could be produced with potato mildew. Somehow the Getty Museum had been blinded by science.[2]

What was the problem? It seems the problem was that the museum *wanted* the kouros to be genuine. The Getty, a young museum, wanted a world-class collection, and the kouros was the perfect piece for that. Somehow that desire compromised their judgment.

One key to deception is a person's intense desire that something is, or is not, true. For example, why did the disciples fail to understand that Jesus was going to die on the cross when Jesus Himself clearly taught that "it was necessary" that the Son of man should "suffer many things . . . and be killed" (Luke 9:22)?[3] In addition, the Gospel of John registers seven references made by Jesus in the last week of His ministry to the "hour" of His death,[4] yet they did not understand. They did not understand because they did not *want* the cross to be true. The difficulty in understanding a biblical truth is often not a matter of the head but of the heart (2 Thessalonians 2:10, 12; 2 Timothy 4:1–4).

The reason the Bible is sometimes difficult to understand is that it requires the reader to abandon cherished desires. It requires conversion. That is why the deep things of God are revealed not to the wise but to the humble: "I thank you, Father, Lord of heaven and earth, that you have hidden these things from the wise and understanding and revealed them to little children; yes, Father, for such was your gracious will" (Matthew 11:25, 26).

The audience's difficulty with the priesthood of Jesus was not a matter of the head but of the heart. They were "dull of hearing" (Hebrews 5:11). They did not want to abandon the beautiful temple of Jerusalem and the glorious, impressive Jewish rituals. They did not want to be branded as turncoats. Pride was producing hearts of unbelief in them,[5] and it could lead them eventually to trample the Son of God underfoot.[6] This implies placing Jesus as a footstool while the believer sits on the throne, just as pride led Lucifer to attempt to sit on the throne and make himself like the Most High.[7]

Salvation is not dependent on knowledge or understanding, but a lack of understanding can be a symptom of a serious spiritual condition. Some people are always learning but unable to arrive at a knowledge of the truth because they accumulate teachers to suit their passions.[8] They do not really love the truth, and that is why they embrace myths and speculations. They will be lost, not for lack of knowledge but because of an unwillingness to embrace a truth that calls them to change.

The Anchor of our faith

The author of Hebrews states that our assurance resides in Jesus Christ. He is "a sure and steadfast anchor of the soul" (Hebrews 6:19). But in what sense does Jesus provide assurance to us?

To answer this question, let us begin by exploring the passage in Hebrews 6. The apostle says that God swore an oath to us in order "to show more convincingly . . . the unchangeable character of his purpose" (verse 17). This is an amazing assertion. Why would God swear an oath to us? Is it not human beings, instead, who have to swear loyalty to God? This passage shows the unbelievable condescendence of God to our fears and doubts. He confirmed the promise of salvation with an oath to help us trust His promise.

The author is referring here to the oath mentioned in Hebrews 5:6: "You are a priest forever, after the order of Melchizedek" (quoting Psalm 110:4). This is clearly shown by the fact that Hebrews 6:20 refers back to that oath and also to the fact that God cannot change His mind. Psalm 110:4 says, "The LORD has sworn and will not change his mind, 'you are a priest forever.'"

God has gone further, however. The author explains that there is not one oath but two oaths to consider: "Two immutable things, in which it is impossible for God to lie" (Hebrews 6:18, NKJV). The author refers to a second oath, the oath God swore to Abraham, which was mentioned in Hebrews 6:13–15.[9] These two oaths—the oaths to Abraham and to David—are different confirmations of God's unbreakable purpose of saving us. Both oaths are unconditional. They do not depend on human faithfulness but on the faithfulness of God. Both oaths are related to the same place—"Zion."[10] Both oaths have as their purpose to bless all humanity.[11] Finally, both oaths were fulfilled through Jesus.[12]

Throughout their history, the oaths to Abraham and David became the ultimate basis of confidence for the people of God. When Moses sought to secure God's forgiveness for the Israelites after they had committed the apostasy of the golden calf and were about to be destroyed, he invoked God's oath to Abraham (Exodus 32:7–14). Similarly, when the psalmist interceded before God for the restoration of Israel, he invoked God's oath to David.[13] The strength of the plea in both cases was that God's oath is irrevocable. God cannot ignore those pleas.[14] Those oaths are "a sure and steadfast anchor of the soul" (Hebrews 6:19).

Thus, God's act of exalting Jesus and seating Him on the throne of the universe at His right hand has enormous significance for human beings. First of all, it demonstrates that God can and will save human beings despite and against Satan's objections (Zechariah 3:1–5; Revelation 12:7–12). Jesus ascended as a human being and as the representative of the human race. His ascension and exaltation demonstrate that God has embraced the whole human race in His person.[15] We have been "accepted in the beloved" (Ephesians 1:6, KJV).

Second, the act of seating Jesus at His right hand affirms God's purpose for human beings. Jesus ascended "as a forerunner in our behalf" (Hebrews 6:20). The love and favor bestowed on Jesus are given as a foretaste of the love and favor God will lavish upon us. We will live with Him (John 14:1–3), sit with Him on the throne (Revelation 3:21), and reign with Him (Revelation 20:6). This is why the author of Hebrews exhorts us to look to Jesus, who is seated at the right hand of God (Hebrews 12:2). Jesus embodies the unchanging nature of God's saving purposes for us. John said that Jesus is the Word of God made flesh (John 1:14; cf. Hebrews 1:1, 2). Hebrews tells us that Jesus is the oath of God incarnated (Hebrews 6:17–20).

This is why we must approach the throne of God with confidence. He has legally bound Himself through oaths sworn before the universe, saying that He will bless us. Hebrews says the oaths are an anchor that enters "within the veil" because that is where God's throne is (verse 19, KJV). The honor of God's rule has been waged on the fulfillment of His promises. The only way God cannot grant our petitions is when they are not done *in* Jesus or when they are not to our benefit.

Thus, we hold fast to Jesus, our Anchor. Holding fast to Jesus means observing Him carefully. He is our Example, and He models how we should live. Holding fast to Jesus also means obeying Him. Obedience is the natural expression of faith. It grows out of our confidence in Him. We obey Him because we have entrusted our lives to Him.

For the believer, obedience is a wonderful experience because it produces true understanding. Hebrews says, "By faith we understand" (Hebrews 11:3). This means that there are truths that believers accept by faith. But there is a deeper sense in this passage. The Greek word for faith (*pistis*) also means faithfulness. Thus, this passage can be translated "by faithfulness we understand." Believers know that faithfulness, or obedience, produces true, deep understanding. They know that when they have faced confusing circumstances, impossible situations, or experiences difficult to understand, and they have stuck to Jesus and obeyed Him, no matter what, He has always delivered. Those experiences have given them a deeper understanding of Jesus' love, power, and faithfulness to His Word. They have come to grasp that the One who created a solution to an impossible, unsolvable problem also created the universe out of nothing. The experience of an obedient life brings a deeper form of knowledge. When we grow in this kind of knowledge, our understanding of Christ improves, our hold on Him strengthens, and our confidence matures.

1. See Félix H. Cortez, "Why the Bible Is So Difficult to Understand," *Perspective Digest* 21, no. 3 (July 1, 2016), https://www.perspectivedigest.org/archive/21-3/why-the-bible-is-so-difficult-to-understand.

2. Malcolm Gladwell, *Blink: The Power of Thinking Without Thinking* (New York: Back Bay Books, 2005), 3–8.

3. Jesus began to teach explicitly about His death once His disciples had settled in the belief that He was the Messiah (Mark 8:29; Matthew 16:15–17; Luke 9:20). First prediction: Mark 8:31; Matthew 16:21; Luke 9:22. Second prediction: Mark 9:31; Matthew 17:22, 23; cf. Luke 9:51, 52. The third was on the last trip to Jerusalem: Mark 10:32–34; Matthew 20:17–19; Luke 18:31–34.

4. John 12:23, 27; 13:1; 16:4, 21, 32; 17:1.

5. Hebrews 3:12; 12:15.

6. Hebrews 10:29.

7. Ezekiel 28:11–19, esp. verse 17; Isaiah 14:13, 14; Ellen G. White, *Patriarchs and Prophets* (Battle Creek, MI: Review and Herald®, 1890), 39.

8. 2 Timothy 3:7; 4:3, 4.

9. Referring to Genesis 22:16–18.

10. Genesis 22:1–18; 1 Chronicles 17:10–14; 2 Chronicles 3:1; Psalms 110:4; 132.

11. Genesis 22:18 (cf. 12:1–3); 2 Samuel 7:18, 19.

12. Luke 1:31–33, 54, 55, 68–75; Acts 2:29–33; 3:24–26; 13:26–35; Galatians 3:7–18.

13. Psalm 89:34–37; cf. verses 38–52.

14. Romans 9:4; 11:28, 29.

15. See Ellen G. White, *The Desire of Ages* (Oakland, CA: Pacific Press®, 1898), 113.

Eight

Jesus, the Mediator of the New Covenant

In the fall of 2016, I experienced a surprising and loving generosity. We had recently moved to the United States, and our financial situation was tight. We could afford only one car, so the children and I walked the short distance to school every day, and my wife drove the car to her job in a nearby town.

We worried about the kids because they had to walk in the snow at night to orchestra practice. We were especially concerned about my daughter because she had to carry her cello. One day while driving home from work, my wife, tired of worrying about the kids, expressed a heartfelt desire: "God, why don't You ask someone to give us a car as a gift?"

A few days later, she and Rocío, a good friend whose birthday is close to hers, went out to celebrate over lunch. As always, they enjoyed a good time. A few days later, Rocío called my wife and asked, "How many cars do you have, Alma?"

"One," she answered. "Why do you ask?"

"Well," Rocío responded, "I just wondered because I always see you in the same car."

"Alma," she continued, "I want to give you my car as a gift. We have decided it. Charlie will buy me a new one."

Alma was stunned by the offer and tried to refuse. "Thank you, but I can't accept it. It is too much."

But Rocío insisted, "Alma, Charlie wants to speak with Felix. Is he there?" My wife handed me the phone. I was initially confused and not sure what to do, but Charlie told me something that has remained in my heart ever since.

"Felix," he said, "I want to ask you something. You are my brother, right?"

"Yes," I told him, "we are brothers. We are good friends."

"Then," he continued, "I want you to accept the car as a gift for Alma. In our family of four, just like yours, we have five cars. It is not right that we have five cars and you have only one. You are my brother. Please, accept the car."

That day Charlie was a mediator and much more. He not only acted as an intercessor but also paid the price for the stunning gift. What Rocío and Charlie did for us illustrates what the Father, the Son, and the Holy Spirit did for humanity and the entire universe.

What is a *covenant*?

A *covenant* is a solemn agreement between two or more parties to do or not to do something. In biblical times, covenants involved an important social dimension: covenants were designed to extend to nonfamily members the protection, financial support, and other benefits that families normally provided. Thus, covenant agreements, both on personal and national levels, used family language to describe the parties and the relationship between them.

Covenants were serious legal affairs. When God made a covenant with Abraham, He asked him to bring four animals and cut them in half.[1] Covenant inscriptions and texts that have survived from antiquity tell us that this was the way covenants were ratified.[2] The sacrifice of the animals served a very important symbolic function. The divided animals represented to the covenant parties their fate should one of them prove unfaithful to the covenant promises.

The covenant between God and Israel was a serious affair. Exodus 24 says that the covenant was ratified with the blood of oxen sprinkled on the twelve pillars representing the people of Israel and on the altar that represented God Himself. It was a covenant of blood. God was trying to say that He would prefer to die before being unfaithful to the promises He had made to the people of Israel and that He expected the same commitment from them. God had liberated them from Egypt and brought them to Himself so that they would be His treasured possession (Exodus 19:4–6). What God did at Sinai when He made a covenant with Israel was to establish a formal process, a legal structure, through which He adopted them as His family. This adoption purpose explains why, after ratifying the covenant with the people of Israel, He asked them to build a house for Him, a sanctuary, so that He could dwell among them (Exodus 25:8).

The covenant that Jesus mediated between God and believers had the purpose of establishing what is probably better described as a family relationship. God, as the Father, would provide protection, guidance, support, and nurture—everything that His children would ever need or want. Believers, on the other hand, return to God their heartfelt love, the only thing they could give, and the only thing God ever wanted.

Interestingly, the covenant between God and Israel illustrates the forces that drive the personal relationship between the believer and God and the cosmic relationships between humanity and God and between the universe and God. All of these relationships, all four levels, are intimately related to each other, just like *matryoshka* dolls are related to each other. They make sense individually but become more beautiful in a set.

How many covenants are there?
God has always structured His relationship with His creatures through covenants. The relationship between God and humanity (Adam) at

Creation was based on a covenant in which God granted humans dominion over the earth and promised to bless them and make them fruitful.[3] Later, God also made covenants with Noah, Abraham, Israel, and David.[4]

But it is important to note that all of these covenants, though distinct from one another because they were made with different individuals, were the expression of a single will and purpose. All of these covenants concretized in specific terms God's original blessing to humanity and His promises of fruitfulness and dominion. For example, God confirmed to Noah the promises made to Adam of fruitfulness and multiplication and of dominion over the animals (Genesis 9:1–17). Similarly, God promised Abraham that He would multiply Abraham's seed like the stars of heaven and the sand of the sea. He would grant them dominion so that they would possess the gate of their enemies. God's purpose was that through them, all the nations of the earth would be blessed (Genesis 22:16–18). To Israel, God promised the He would set it high above all the nations of the earth and make it extremely prosperous and fruitful (Deuteronomy 28:1–14). In the same way, God promised to make David's royal descendant the highest of the kings of the earth and give him dominion over his enemies (Psalm 89:22, 23, 25–27). The fact that all of these covenants contain the same promises and the same purpose of blessing for creation suggests that they are all instantiations of a single eternal will and purpose; that is, they are historical manifestations of a single eternal covenant.[5]

The covenants reveal, then, who God is.[6] First, they reveal God's generosity and grace. He has forgiven the transgressions of His creatures and provided what they need to return to a full relationship with Him. Second, they reveal God's uniqueness. All covenants between humans are subject to the whims of human power and ability. They are also subject to the fickleness of their purpose. God's promises and purposes, however, remain forever fixed because He lives forever. His power and ability are limitless, and His purpose is unchangeable.

Adam and Eve, Noah, Abraham, Israel, and the lineage of David all broke their promises and covenant commitments, yet God remained faithful to them because He is a God of steadfast love who keeps His covenants (Deuteronomy 7:9; 2 Timothy 2:13).

But God's covenant relationship with His creation has never been dependent on the creatures' faithfulness. Creatures cannot carry that responsibility. From eternity past, before the ages began, Jesus offered to guarantee the covenant through His obedience and sacrifice. The Son covenanted with the Father that He would underwrite the covenantal obligations of the creatures and restore them to righteousness should they fall.[7] And that is what He did.

Hebrews 8–10 focuses on how God restored the covenant relationship with His people. These chapters explore the covenant established at Mount Sinai after the Exodus, the golden calf apostasy, Israel's spotty faithfulness, and God's renewal of the covenant through Jesus.

The old covenant

Hebrews 8:6, 7 says that Jesus has mediated a new covenant that is more excellent because the first, or old, covenant was defective. The apostle explains in verses 8 and 9 that the old covenant was defective because the people did not continue in it. Thus, the problem was the people, not the covenant itself. In Hebrews 7, however, the apostle mentions a limitation that the old covenant had that we need to explore further. The apostle explained that the old covenant was weak and useless because it was unable to provide perfection; that is to say, it could not provide the true cleansing of the conscience that would make it possible for believers to approach God (verses 18, 19).[8] What, then, did this old, or first, covenant stipulate, and why was it weak?

Hebrews 7:11 says that Israel received the law based on the Levitical priesthood (NASB). The apostle is not referring to the covenant inaugurated in Exodus 20–24 but to the renewal of that covenant relationship between God and Israel *after* the golden calf apostasy in Exodus 32–34, which was when the Levitical priesthood was established. The renewal of the covenant in Exodus 32–34 involved the confirmation of the Ten Commandments (Exodus 34:1) but also the addition of laws that consisted mostly of ritual and cultic regulations (verses 11–26), which, intriguingly, also numbered ten. The cult and ritual regulations pointed forward to the ministry and sacrifice of Jesus (Hebrews 10:1–4) and were the basis upon which the original covenant relationship between God and Israel was renewed (Exodus 34:27).[9] Their purpose was to provide Israel with safeguards and protection.

For the apostle, then, the old, or first, covenant is the covenant renewed between Israel and God after the golden calf apostasy, based on the additional ritual and cultic laws. Therefore, and this is important, Hebrews is not comparing the new covenant mediated by Jesus to the original covenant between God and Israel at Sinai (Exodus 20–24). Hebrews is comparing, instead, two renewals of the same original covenant at Sinai. On the one hand, there is the renewal of the covenant by Moses after the golden calf apostasy, based on the mediation of Levitical priests and the addition of ritual and cultic laws (Exodus 32–34). On the other hand, there is the renewal of the covenant by Jesus, based on His eternal priesthood and His "once for all" sacrifice (Hebrews 9:11–10:18).

Both Moses and Jesus renewed the original covenant between God and Israel at Sinai (Exodus 20–24) but with different results. Moses' covenant renewal was temporary. Its function was important because it pointed forward to the solution provided by Jesus. But when Jesus came, the covenant would become obsolete and ready to vanish away (Hebrews 8:13). Thus, Moses' covenant regulations reminded the people that God's cleansing or forgiveness was not achieved by the sacrifices themselves but by the future work of God on their behalf through the Messiah. Sadly, many people failed to look beyond the sacrifices to the ultimate reality of the Messiah's sacrifice.

The new covenant

God sent Jesus to this world as the Messenger of the covenant (Malachi 3:1) to restore the relationship between God and His people. That is to say, Jesus came to Earth to establish the new covenant.

The covenant between God and Israel had been broken and renewed under the same provisions several times because the nation had lapsed time and again into apostasy,[10] and it had become painfully clear that the people were simply unable to keep the conditions of their covenant with God (Jeremiah 13:23). Thus, God promised to do a "new thing" (Jeremiah 31:22).[11] He would put His law "within them," enabling them to obey (verse 33). God did not change His law or lower His standards. Instead, He changed the condition of the people, ensuring the success of the covenant. This new covenant is unique. It does not have curses because it will never be broken. It only has blessings.

The document of the first covenant had been written by God on two tables of stone and deposited in the ark of the covenant as an important witness of God's covenant with His people (Exodus 31:18; 34:27; Deuteronomy 4:13; 5:22; 10:1–4).[12] But documents written in stone can be broken, and scrolls, as Jeremiah experienced, can be burned, drowned, lost, or ignored.[13] But God promised to do a new thing. He would write His law in the hearts of the people, where it cannot be lost or ignored.

Jeremiah had pointed out that the problem of Israel was that its sin was engraved "with a pen of iron; with a point of diamond . . . on the tablet of their heart" (Jeremiah 17:1). The people had stubborn hearts (Jeremiah 13:10; 23:17; 12:1); therefore, it was impossible for them to do the right thing (Jeremiah 13:23). They needed heart surgery (Jeremiah 4:4). Thus, God promised to inscribe His law in their hearts to promote obedience (Psalms 40:8; 119:11; cf. Deuteronomy 11:18).[14]

The laws God will write in His people's hearts are more than the law God gave Israel at Sinai. The Ten Commandments are "the foundational layer of Yahweh's expectation" for His people.[15] In addition to this foundational layer, God wants to inscribe in the heart of His people the total declaration of His will.[16] He wants His people to be able to live in full agreement with His will.

The new covenant also promises that God will forgive the sins of His people. This promise refers to much more than merely absolving believers from any crimes they may have committed. God promises that He will "remember their sins no more" (Hebrews 8:12), which implies the restoration of the relationship between Him and His people. Similarly, God promises that He will clean the conscience of His people from any sin (Hebrews 9:14; 10:1–4, 22), which will give them the confidence, even boldness, to approach Him with "full assurance of faith" (Hebrews 10:22).

---

1. Genesis 15:7–16; Ellen G. White, *Patriarchs and Prophets* (Battle Creek, MI: Review and Herald®, 1890), 137.

2. Gerhard F. Hasel, "The Meaning of the Animal Rite in Genesis 15," *Journal for the Study of the Old Testament* 6, no. 19 (February 1981): 61–78.

3. Genesis 1:26–28; Hosea 6:7; Jeremiah 33:19, 20.

4. Noah: Genesis 6:18; 9:1–17. Abraham: Genesis 15:7–21; 17:1–27; 22:15–19; cf. 12:1–3. Israel: Exodus 20–24; Leviticus 26:3–45; Deuteronomy 27–30; 2 Samuel 7:4–17; 1 Chronicles 17:3–15.

5. White, *Patriarchs and Prophets*, 370, 371.

6. E.g., Exodus 6:2–8; Deuteronomy 4:32–40; 7:7–10. See John H. Walton, *Covenant: God's Purpose, God's Plan* (Grand Rapids, MI: Zondervan, 1994), 24–46.

7. Colossians 1:16, 17; cf. Matthew 25:34, 41; Acts 2:23; Romans 16:25; 1 Corinthians 2:7; Ephesians 1:3–6; 2 Timothy 1:9; Titus 1:2; 1 Peter 1:18–20.

8. Cf. Hebrews 9:9, 10; 10:1–4.

9. This suggests that Moses wrote the additional commandments in another place (Exodus 34:27) and that God Himself wrote the Ten Commandments on the tablets of stone brought by Moses (Exodus 34:28 [here, God is the subject]; cf. verse 1; Deuteronomy 10:4).

10. The covenant had been renewed in the days of Asa (2 Chronicles 15:10–15), Jehoiada (2 Kings 11:17), Hezekiah (2 Chronicles 29:10), and Josiah (2 Kings 23:3).

11. In this, he agrees with the tenor of the promises of restoration in the prophets: Isaiah 43:19; 48:6; 62:2; 65:17; Ezekiel 11:19; 18:31; 36:26.

12. The tablets of stone contained the Ten Commandments and were deposited in the ark. Exodus 24:7 also refers to the book of the covenant, which included the instructions in Exodus 20:22–23:33. This book was probably placed beside the ark, just as the book of the law that contained the renovation of the covenant in Moab was (Deuteronomy 31:26).

13. Broken: Exodus 32:19; Deuteronomy 9:17. Burned: Jeremiah 36:23. Drowned: Jeremiah 51:63. Lost or ignored: 2 Kings 22:8.

14. Thus, Jeremiah and Ezekiel refer elsewhere to a "new heart" and a "new spirit" given to the people (Ezekiel 18:31; 36:26; cf. Jeremiah 24:7; 32:39; Ezekiel 11:19). New Testament authors refer to this action by God as "regeneration" or "rebirth" (John 1:10–13; 3:1–10; Titus 3:5; 1 Peter 1:3, 23; 1 John 4:7; 5:18).

15. John I. Durham, *Exodus*, Word Biblical Commentary, vol. 3 (Waco, TX: Word, 1987), 300.

16. F. García López and Heinz-Josef Fabry, "תּוֹרָה," in *Theological Dictionary of the Old Testament*, vol. 15 (Grand Rapids, MI: Eerdmans, 2015), 626.

Nine

Jesus,
the Perfect Sacrifice

The first symbols we find repeatedly in Christian paintings in cata-combs include the peacock,[1] dove, athlete's victory palm, and fish.[2] Later, other themes appeared: Noah's ark, Abraham sacrificing the ram instead of Isaac, Daniel in the lions' den, Jonah being spit out by the fish, a shepherd carrying a lamb, the healing of the paralytic, and the raising of Lazarus. All of these pictures were symbols representing salvation, victory, and care. On the other hand, the cross appeared later and conveyed a sense of defeat and shame, inviting derision from both Jews and pagans (Hebrews 12:2; Galatians 5:11). It posed a challenge for the preaching of the gospel. It was counterintuitive and difficult to explain.[3] Yet, the cross became the emblem of Christianity.[4] Why?

The Cross was central to Jesus' preaching and to the apostles' preaching. In fact, Paul simply called the gospel "the word of the cross" (1 Corinthians 1:18). Today, the Cross remains the focal point of the Christian gospel because it represents three important accomplishments of the Messiah.

Jesus defeated the devil at the cross
The Cross represents the defeat of Satan. In the wake of Adam's sin,

God's purpose for man was thwarted, and humanity was doomed. Romans 5:12–21 says that because of one man's sin, death reigned over all humans because all sinned. Like an infectious disease, Adam's transgression was transmitted to all of humanity, and the children of Adam had no resources to fight it. Thus, humankind was subjugated under the power of evil.[5]

Death reigns because humanity is powerless before sin. Satan rules over us by tempting us, deceiving us, and accusing us, bringing death as a result. In this sense, he has the power of death (Hebrews 2:14).[6] God, however, gave us life "by canceling the record of debt that stood against us with its legal demands. This he set aside, nailing it to the cross. He disarmed the rulers and authorities and put them to open shame, by triumphing over them in him" (Colossians 2:14, 15). Jesus stripped Satan of his weapons by living a perfect life and satisfying the legal demands against us. The Bible teaches that Satan's defeat and God's ability to forgive sin result from Jesus' victory at the cross.

Jesus propitiated the wrath of God at the cross

Scripture also asserts that Jesus satisfied the wrath of God. Jesus was hanged on a tree (the cross), which, according to Deuteronomy 21:23, meant that Jesus died under God's curse. Jesus described His death on the cross as *a cup* He had to drink (Matthew 26:39),[7] symbolizing God's judgment upon the wicked.[8]

But why did Jesus die as a convicted criminal under the judgment of God if He committed no sin?[9] Hebrews 9:15 explains that Jesus died to redeem humans from the transgressions they had committed. He suffered God's wrath in their place.[10] Ironically, this act of bearing our sin reveals the divine identity of Jesus because, in the Old Testament, only God can bear our sins and forgive them (Exodus 32:32; Isaiah 43:24, 25; 53:4, 6).[11]

We may wonder why God did not simply forgive Adam and Eve when they sinned, just as He asks His children to forgive when they are offended.[12] The problem is that Adam's sin was more than a personal affront against God. It was a challenge to God's rule and the moral order of the universe. In the end, the existence of order in the universe depends on the divine reaction to a breach of that order. God cannot tolerate sin, just as a loving father cannot tolerate a deadly virus to exist in his home. Thus, God's love for creation requires the destruction of evil.

Jesus revealed who God is at the cross

The Cross demonstrated God's love for us. Hebrews 10:20 says that through His sacrifice, Jesus opened a "new and living way . . . through the curtain"; that is, He provided access for us to the presence of God. The inner curtain of the sanctuary represented the separation between God and His children. It separated the ark of the covenant—where God's glorious presence was manifested—from the rest of the sanctuary. Only the high priest could enter there and then only once a year (Leviticus 16:1–3; Hebrews 9:6, 7). When Jesus died, however, the veil of the temple was torn in two, and the Most Holy Place was revealed (Matthew 27:51). This was a powerful symbol that the Cross had somehow given us the possibility to look more closely into God Himself.

Jesus affirmed that the Cross would reveal the glory of God and His Son.[13] Similarly, Paul asserted that God gave His Son to die on the cross to demonstrate both His righteousness and His love—that is, to reveal His character (Romans 3:25, 26). The Cross was a revelatory act.

By revealing the depth of His love and righteousness through Jesus' death on the cross, God got to the bottom of the problem of sin—to its very root. The serpent had affirmed at the tree of the knowledge of good and evil that God was not as loving as He claimed to be and that He was selfishly retaining a benefit that was rightfully humanity's. The serpent also implied that God was not as righteous or truthful as He said He was.

At its root, the problem of evil is a distrust of God, His motives, and His actions. But Jesus cleared God's name (John 12:27, 28). At the cross, He demonstrated that God loves us, is loyal to us, and is committed to justice and truth, even at the cost of His own life. He also demonstrated the true nature of His government. His rule consists of love, righteousness, and abnegation. This is why there is power and wisdom in the cross (1 Corinthians 1:18–31). The love and righteousness demonstrated there compel us in ways that nothing else could (2 Corinthians 5:14).

Jesus' sacrifice and our sacrifices

Had I been born in a traditional Mexican home, my name would have been Guadalupe. I was born around 10:00 P.M. on Friday, December 12, which is the Day of the Virgin of Guadalupe. I was born, however, in the home of an Adventist pastor and in the clinic of Dr. Elías Tinoco, an Adventist doctor. I was given a biblical middle name, taken from the list of Israelites that returned from Babylon to rebuild Jerusalem, because my parents sought to instill in my brothers and me the desire to always be one of those who "raise up the foundations of many generations" and are called "repairer of the breach" (Isaiah 58:12). I was also registered as having been born on December 13 because, according to the Bible, Friday night is already the Sabbath.

December 12 has long held a fascination for me. According to tradition, the virgin of Guadalupe appeared for the fourth time to Juan Diego on this date in 1531, asking him that a church be built for her on the hill of Tepeyac.[14] The Basilica of Guadalupe was built in that place and is visited by around twenty million people every year. It is the third-most-visited sacred site in the world.[15] My first home as a pastor was one block from Calzada Zaragoza, the main entrance to Mexico City from the east, which was crowded with pilgrims on the days preceding December 12. Many came *pagar sus mandas* (to fulfill their vows). These *mandas* are sacrifices promised to the virgin of Guadalupe in exchange for a miracle or a favor. One of the most popular *mandas* is going on your knees or barefoot for long distances to the Basilica of Guadalupe. Other popular *mandas* involve deprivation of food or sexual relations or the giving of offerings.

I saw many people perform these *mandas*. It always saddened me to think that, despite their sincerity, their privations and sufferings were not only unnecessary but also harmful. Scripture says that on the cross, Jesus made a sacrifice that is "once for all."[16] This expression means that the merits of Jesus' death on the cross are effective for everyone, for every sin, and for every favor.[17] Its value and power surpass and overwhelm our ability to understand it. Our sacrifices are as unnecessary as lighting a candle to assist the sun on a cloudless day.

When we insist on bringing our sacrifices, we unwittingly reveal that in the depth of our hearts, Jesus' sacrifice is not enough—at least not enough for our huge sin. Jesus feels the sting of our unintended contempt, but He does not hold it against us.

But there is a more sinister reason that our sacrifices are harmful. Any sacrifice brought before God to merit His favor or His forgiveness originates and reinforces a transactional attitude. It reinforces the belief that the forgiveness and favors we receive from God must be repaid. Transactional Christians believe that God is like a banker: He grants us a loan in our time of need and helps us live when nobody else is willing. Transactional Christians recognize God's forbearance as He waits patiently when we delay in paying back the obedient and faithful service He deserves. Transactional Christians may even consider God a loving and patient banker, yet He is still a banker for them, nonetheless. We reveal a transactional Christianity when we continually count the cost and the sacrifices we have made; when we offer faithful service and obedience in exchange for favors; when our religion is based mainly on promises, honor, commitment, and responsibility; or when we insist on paying back the gift.

Insisting on paying back a gift is a polite way of rejecting that gift. Parents, lovers, and friends rejoice in giving and receiving gifts. As they give a gift, they keenly observe the face of the person receiving it, trying to capture the moment. They want to be sure not to miss the recipient's reaction of surprise and joy and the embrace that comes afterward. Some even record it on video to relive at a later time. That is all the reward they are looking for. Anything less is a failure.

On the other hand, the receiving party receives it with open arms, celebrates it, shows it with pride, revels in it, and treasures it. The acceptance of a gift implies accepting the strong bonds of friendship, kinship, or love. Sometimes, however, accepting a gift implies accepting a relationship we do not want because we feel unworthy or because we cannot trust that relationship. Abraham harbored a measure of distrust when he returned the gift of the king of Sodom (Genesis 14:21–24). He preferred a relationship that was not too close.

But God wants a close relationship with His children. He loves us deeply and lives for those moments when we are surprised by His love and our face lights up with sincere joy. He loves those moments. They make His face shine. When we insist on paying back those gifts, however, He feels the sting of rejection. He endures it patiently but feels the sorrow of being misunderstood and the pain of an arm's length relationship.

Of course, genuine believers offer sacrifices. God encourages His children to present their bodies as "a living sacrifice, holy and acceptable to God" and to offer sacrifices of praise, of doing good, and of sharing what they have because "such sacrifices are pleasing" to Him.[18] Those sacrifices, however, are different. They are not attempts to supplement the sacrifice of Jesus or to pay Him back. The believer praises God, confesses His name, shares what he has, and shares in Jesus' suffering because it is his privilege to do so.[19] The believer is not repaying God for His mercy but simply extending that mercy to others. He has entered a new relationship—a new partnership in which it is his privilege to imitate Jesus and advance His cause. He has experienced the joy of salvation and wants to share in the joy of redeeming humans.

1. The peacock supposedly symbolizes immortality.

2. The Greek word for fish, *ichthys*, was an acronym for *Iesus Christos Theou Huios Soter*, meaning "Jesus Christ, Son of God, Savior."

3. 1 Corinthians 1:18, 23.

4. Félix H. Cortez, "What Did Jesus Accomplish on the Cross?," in *God's Character and the Last Generation*, ed. Jiří Moskala and John C. Peckham (Nampa, ID: Pacific Press®, 2018), 174, 175.

5. Romans 7:14–25; 2 Corinthians 4:4; Ephesians 2:2; Colossians 1:13; 1 John 5:19.

6. Jeremy R. Treat argues that "the reign of Satan therefore is parasitic to the reign of sin (Romans 5:21)." *The Crucified King: Atonement and Kingdom in Biblical and Systematic Theology* (Grand Rapids, MI: Zondervan, 2014), 199–203.

7. Cf. Mark 14:36; Luke 22:42; John 18:11.

8. When God confronted Israel because of its unfaithfulness and wickedness, He warned that it would drink the cup of His wrath (Ezekiel 23:32–34). See also Psalm 75:8; Job 21:20; Jeremiah 6:30; 7:29; 8:9; 14:19; Revelation 14:9–11; 15:7–16:21.

9. Hebrews 2:17, 18; 4:15; 7:26–28; 9:14.

10. According to Scripture, Jesus bore the ultimate penalty for sin in our stead (Romans 5:6, 8; 2 Corinthians 5:21; Galatians 3:13) and experienced in our place the eternal punishment reserved for the wicked (1 Timothy 2:5, 6; Titus 2:14; 1 John 2:2).

11. In the original of Exodus 32:32, to *forgive* means literally that God bears our sins.

12. Matthew 18:21–35; Mark 11:25; Luke 6:37; 17:3, 4.

13. John 12:23–28; 13:31–35; 17:1; cf. 3:14; 12:32.

14. For a story of the controversy and doubts about the veracity of the apparitions, see Stafford Poole, *The Guadalupan Controversies in Mexico* (Stanford, CA: Stanford University Press, 2006). The historical veracity of the apparitions of the virgin of Guadalupe has been doubted by Catholic clerics from early times to the present. Guillermo von Schulenburg Prado, the abbot of the Basilica of Guadalupe, openly doubted the historicity of Juan Diego and opposed his canonization in 1996.

15. April Orcutt, "World's Most-Visited Sacred Sites," BBC, January 24, 2012, http://www.bbc.com/travel/story/20120124-worlds-most-visited-sacred-sites.

16. Romans 6:10; Hebrews 7:27; 9:12, 26, 28; 10:2, 10.

17. John 1:29; 3:16; 1 John 2:2.

18. Romans 12:1; Hebrews 13:15, 16; 1 Peter 2:5.

19. 2 Corinthians 1:5; Philippians 3:10; Hebrews 13:13; 1 Peter 4:13.

Ten

Jesus Opens a Way Through the Veil

In 1892, Homer Plessy deliberately violated Louisiana's Separate Car Act of 1890. This law required "separate but equal" car accommodations for white and nonwhite passengers. Plessy, a person of seven-eighths white and one-eighth black ancestry, violated the law when he boarded a "whites only" train car. Plessy was arrested, tried, and convicted in New Orleans, but he appealed through the courts of the state of Louisiana to the US Supreme Court. The US Supreme Court reviewed the case in 1896, known as *Plessy v. Ferguson*, and concluded that racial segregation laws for public facilities were constitutional as long as the segregated facilities were equal in quality. This landmark decision was the basis for much of the Jim Crow laws that enforced racial segregation in the southern United States for almost a century. This state of affairs was finally overturned with the Civil Rights Act of 1964 that outlawed discrimination based on race, color, religion, sex, and national origin. The history of racial segregation in the southern states and the long struggle by the civil rights movement to provide African Americans with equal access to rights and privileges suggest that the notion of "separate but equal" is untenable. There is no equality if there is no parity of access.

Human beings were also excluded for a long time from access to the full benefits of the government of God and to His presence. Adam and Eve were evicted from the Garden of Eden and barred from the tree of life. Their alienation from God led them to ignorance, moral destitution, enslavement to the devil, and finally, death. Our situation, however, was not the result of unjustified divine discrimination or unfairness. It was the result of our own choices.

The reason I have introduced the achievements of the civil rights movement as an illustration resides not in the similarities it provides to Jesus' achievement for humanity but in the contrasts it yields. The civil rights movement was a social endeavor that progressed from the bottom to the top. In other words, those who were affected by discrimination organized and struggled to obtain equal access at the cost of great personal sacrifice. Jesus' achievement, however, was the result of a movement that progressed from the top to the bottom. The Godhead organized to restore humanity's access to the full benefits of the government of God and His presence, despite humanity joining with Satan to overturn God's rule on Earth. The cost of this struggle was enormous, and all of heaven became involved in the work to save humankind (Hebrews 1:14). God Himself paid the greatest price when He died on the cross in the person of the Son in order to restore humanity to full and confident access to God.[1]

"Show me your glory"

Israel's worship of the golden calf at Mount Sinai was similar in its significance and consequence to Adam and Eve's sin in the Garden of Eden. God did not immediately destroy Israel but chose to suspend the punishment, just as He had done with Adam and Eve. Yet the Israelites' sin caused God to cast them from His presence: "The LORD said to Moses, 'Depart; go up from here, you and the people whom you have brought up out of the land of Egypt. . . . I will send an angel before you. . . . But I will not go up among you, lest I consume you on the way, for you are a stiff-necked people' " (Exodus 33:1–3). The tent that served as a temporary place to worship God was removed from the camp and pitched outside, far off from the camp (verse 7).

This was a disastrous development, and Moses knew that Israel did not have a chance without God's presence. So he interceded: "If your presence will not go with me, do not bring us up from here" (verse 15). God heard Moses' supplication and promised to go with them (verse 17). But Moses thirsted for a greater token of God's favor. "Please show me your glory," he asked (verse 18). Moses knew that granting access to the representative of a sinful people was the surest token of God's favor.

God granted Moses what he could endure, but this was not yet the restoration of favor that God wanted for Israel: " 'I will make all my goodness pass before you and will proclaim before you my name. . . . But,' he said, 'you cannot see my face, for man shall not see me and live.'. . . 'I will put you in a cleft of the rock, and I will cover you with my hand until I have passed by. Then I will take away my hand, and you shall see my back, but my face shall not be seen' " (verses 19, 20, 22, 23). He also arranged for the tabernacle to be built where He would dwell literally in the midst of Israel; yet the tabernacle would be pitched in the center of a hollow square formed by the camp of Israel, two-thirds of a mile (or two thousand cubits) from the nearest Israelite tent.[2] The tribe of Levi would camp around the tabernacle as guardians to prevent any Israelite, under the penalty of death, from trespassing its sacred limits (Numbers 1:53; 3:7–10, 38).

God's presence and glory in the camp of Israel were always guarded by a protective veil, be it the hand of God protecting Moses, the inner curtain of the sanctuary as a protecting barrier for the priests, or the Levites as a protecting wall of the sanctuary for Israel. These protective veils were the continuation of the flaming sword that prevented access to the tree of life in the Garden of Eden (Genesis 3:24). But all of these veils, from Eden to the Exodus, would eventually be taken away through the ministry of Jesus Christ.

The new and living VIP pass

Jesus' death, resurrection, and ascension were the pivotal moments in God's long and sustained effort to restore humanity to communion with Him. The first evidence of this change was seen at His baptism. The heavens were torn open, and for the first time since the proclamation of the Ten Commandments at Mount Sinai, God spoke directly and audibly to the assembly. Through Jesus, the veil was opened.

Moses saw a glimpse of God's glory, but Jesus was "the radiance of the glory of God" (Hebrews 1:3). In Jesus, God Himself became flesh, and we saw His glory, "glory as of the only Son from the Father, full of grace and truth" (John 1:14). Later on, when Jesus died on the cross, "the curtain of the temple was torn in two, from top to bottom" (Matthew 27:51), symbolizing that Jesus had torn apart the veil that separated us from God.

Jesus did not change God's attitude toward humanity. His life and death were simply the next steps in bringing us back into harmony with God. Through Jesus, God provided cleansing for our sins and the sins of the whole world, giving us the confidence to enter into His presence (Hebrews 10:1–4, 10–14, 19–22).

"Within the veil"

Adventists are often confused regarding the identity of the veil through which Jesus entered when He ascended to the heavenly sanctuary. In fact, this is one of the questions students most often ask me: Where exactly in the heavenly sanctuary did Jesus enter when He ascended?

Hebrews 6:19, 20 says that Jesus entered "within the veil" "as a forerunner for us" (NASB). Referring to the same event, Hebrews 10:20 says that Jesus inaugurated for us "a new and living way . . . through the veil [*katapetasma*]" (NASB). Of course, the author of Hebrews is referring to the veil of the heavenly sanctuary, which Jesus entered at His ascension.[3]

Ellen White describes Jesus' ascension to the heavenly sanctuary as corresponding to the entrance of the high priest into the Holy of Holies.

As in the typical service the high priest laid aside his pontifical robes and officiated in the white linen dress of an ordinary priest; so Christ laid aside His royal robes and garbed Himself with humanity and offered sacrifice, Himself the priest, Himself the victim. As the high priest, after performing his service in the holy of holies, came forth to the waiting congregation in his pontifical robes; so Christ will come the second time, clothed in garments of whitest white, "so as no fuller on earth can white them." Mark 9:3. He will come in His own glory, and in the glory of His Father, and all the angelic host will escort Him on His way.[4]

What Hebrews and Ellen White are saying is that Jesus has complete, unimpeded access to the presence of God, which earthly priests could only dream of.

Three veils
The earthly sanctuary, "a copy and shadow" of the heavenly sanctuary (Hebrews 8:5), had three veils (*katapetasma*): the screen of the court that served as an entrance into the court,[5] the screen at the entrance of the outer room of the sanctuary,[6] and the inner veil that separated the outer room (Holy Place) from the inner room (Most Holy Place).[7] The phrase "within the veil" (*esōteron tou katapetasmatos*) appears four times in the Septuagint and consistently denotes the Holy of Holies, or Most Holy Place, of the sanctuary.[8] This phrase is used in Hebrews 6:19, which would suggest that Jesus entered into the Holy of Holies of the heavenly sanctuary. In the earthly sanctuary, the priests would die if they entered "within the veil" into the Holy of Holies. Only the high priest could enter into the Holy of Holies once a year after going through strict preparations and with the protection of the cloud of incense (Leviticus 16:1–3, 12, 13). Jesus, however, has permanent access to the very presence of God, "within the veil" of the heavenly sanctuary (Hebrews 10:11–14).

But the references to the veil in Hebrews do not make sense if they are taken as spatial pointers inside the heavenly sanctuary. Hebrews 10:19, 20 says that we are now able to enter the heavenly sanctuary by the "new and living way . . . through the veil" (NASB) that Jesus opened for us. Since the sanctuary has only one door, it is impossible to enter the sanctuary precinct through the inner veil. It would be similar to saying that we entered a bank through the door of the vault. If we wanted to describe the movements of Jesus spatially, we would have to identify the veil of Hebrews 10:20 as the outer veil—the one that leads first into the outer room of the sanctuary.[9]

The references to the veil in Hebrews suggest that the descriptions of Jesus' passage through the veil have a theological significance rather than a physical one. There are at least three aspects of this theological significance.

First, Jesus' entrance "within the veil" testifies to the efficacy of Jesus' sacrifice (verses 19, 20) and to the sinless perfection of His character (Hebrews 6:19, 20; cf. 4:15; 5:9, 10; 7:26–28). Only a sinless being can be in the immediate presence of God (Hebrews 4:15; 7:26–28).

Second, Jesus' entrance "within the veil" signals the greatness of His achievement (Hebrews 8:1). Jesus, our Representative, was not simply granted access to the heavenly court. He sits on the throne with God. No one is closer to the center of power in the universe than Jesus.

Finally, Jesus' entrance "within the veil" tells us about the depth of God's love. He has brought near the race that once rebelled against Him.

When my children were still young, I often had to travel on weekends. When I returned from those trips, they wanted to sleep with me. They would flip a coin to decide who was going to sleep with me the first night. They wanted to be close to their father.

In God's case, He longs to be close to His children. Like a father who tightly embraces a child who was lost, God will eagerly move His throne to Earth, forever living close to His children (Revelation 21; 22). This utopia is only made possible by Jesus Christ, a living VIP pass that has no expiration date!

1. Hebrews 10:19–23; 4:14–16; John 1:12; Galatians 4:4–7.

2. Joshua 3:3, 4; Midrash on Numbers Rabbah, 2:9.

3. Hebrews 4:14 says that Jesus went "through the heavens" into the third heaven (implied; cf. Hebrews 9:24), where the heavenly sanctuary is located (Hebrews 8:1, 2; 9:8, 12, 24; 10:19; 13:11).

4. Ellen G. White, *The Acts of the Apostles* (Mountain View, CA: Pacific Press®, 1911), 33.

5. E.g., Exodus 38:18.

6. E.g., Exodus 36:37; 26:36, 37.

7. E.g., Exodus 26:31, 33, 34, 35.

8. Exodus 26:33; Leviticus 16:2, 12, 15; cf. Numbers 18:7. See Roy E. Gane, "Re-opening *Katapetasma* ("Veil") in Hebrews 6:19," *Andrews University Seminary Studies* 38, no. 1 (Spring 2000): 5–8.

9. Ellen G. White identifies the veil of Hebrews 6:19 with the curtain that provided entrance to the outer room and the sanctuary as a whole (*The Great Controversy* [Mountain View, CA: Pacific Press®, 1911], 420, 421). It is also possible to understand that the heavenly sanctuary has only one room, the Holy of Holies, which would fit the description of the heavenly Jerusalem as the tabernacle of God, with the cubic proportions of the Holy of Holies of the sanctuary. Interestingly, Hebrews does not refer to the outer room of the heavenly sanctuary. Hebrews does not, however, deny the existence of an outer room in the heavenly sanctuary. Thus, our description of the physical nature of the heavenly sanctuary must remain tentative.

I also would like to point out that Ellen G. White's description of the vision in which she saw the Father and then Jesus go through the veil into the Holy of Holies in 1844 should not be taken as a literal, physical description of Jesus' movement from one room to the other of the heavenly sanctuary (*Early Writings* [Battle Creek, MI: Review and Herald®, 1882], 55). Ellen G. White clearly explained later that her vision should not be interpreted literally (White, 92). She noted that she observed in that vision human beings in their mortal state, and even Satan, as present in the heavenly sanctuary and that could not be interpreted literally. The vision was symbolic, just as the vision we find in chapter 12 of Revelation.

Finally, it is important to say that the heavenly sanctuary is real, even if we do not know about its details. The heavenly sanctuary is not simply a metaphor. The earthly sanctuary was made according to the model of the heavenly sanctuary shown to Moses on the mountain (Exodus 25:40; Hebrews 8:5). Furthermore, the heavenly sanctuary must be of such a nature that the Son of God, in human nature, could enter into it. In fact, we will enter into it at the end of time.

Eleven

Jesus, Author and Perfecter of Our Faith

When Hadid, my oldest son, was eight or nine years old, he became worried when he knew that his cousin Gianni was sick and had to be taken to the hospital. Hadid thought that his young cousin was going to die. I tried to reassure him by saying that the doctors would give him the treatment he needed, and more important, we were going to ask God to help him heal. But my son was not comforted. "Dad," he told me, "do not pray. God does not answer prayer."

"Why do you say that?" I asked him.

"I prayed for Elann, and God did not answer," he responded.

Elann was my youngest son who died after battling cancer for several months. Hadid was seven years old when his seven-month-old little brother died. He loved him dearly and prayed for him fervently. I remember that he was present when our family and friends met at the hospital to anoint little Elann. I also remember the sad moment a few days later when I told him that we were taking Elann home because nobody could do anything and only a miracle could heal him. He cried for a long time, and I could not comfort him. I think he sensed that his mother and I continued to pray constantly for Elann. He was probably unaware that his grandmother had asked that we allow her to take care of the baby for a night and that she had held the baby in her arms and prayed all night long, asking God to heal him. When Elann died, Hadid seemed calm. He and his little sister held Elann in their arms for a while before Elann was taken to the funeral home. I did not realize it then, but at that moment, something broke inside Hadid, and he lost his faith.

Hadid did not rebel. He continued to read his Bible every day and do his homework. He attended church with us and paid attention, but we noticed that he stopped singing and did not close his eyes during prayer. Around that time, at the end of a study on the meaning of baptism for his Bible class, Mom, who homeschooled him, asked him whether he would like to be baptized in the future. He said he could not because one needs to have faith to be baptized, and he did not have faith. He also explained that he could understand that God did not have an end, but he could not understand that God did not have a beginning. Of the many questions he asked me, however, the one that stuck in my mind was, *"Dad, how do you really know that Jesus is going to come back again?"*

By the way, friend, how do you really know that Jesus is coming again? Is there any concrete, objective evidence that Jesus will return? Or is faith simply an attitude we have toward God and His promises? Does the fact that you and I believe those promises make them real? Is there really a qualitative difference between our trust in what the Bible says and the trust QAnon followers have in the "drops" of Q on the web? Is the only difference between the followers of David Koresh and us their unfortunate choice of following the wrong leader and embracing the wrong interpretations of the Bible? What is *faith*? What does it mean to have faith?

Faith does not have a better reputation today than it had in ancient times.[1] From the point of view of classical Greek philosophy, faith was the lowest level of cognition. "It was the state of mind of the uneducated."[2] Galen, who was relatively sympathetic to Christianity, said that Christians possessed three of the four cardinal virtues: they had courage, self-control, and justice but lacked *phronēsis* (intellectual insight), which, in his opinion, was the rational basis for the other three.[3] Others were less favorable. Celsus accused them of being enemies of science. In his opinion, Christians were frauds who deceived people by saying that knowledge is bad for the health of the soul.[4] Porphyry repeated Celsus's accusation, protesting "an irrational and unexamined *pistis* [faith],"[5] and Julian blurted out, "There is nothing in your philosophy beyond the one word 'Believe!' "[6] James W. Thompson has noted that "a catalogue of heroes of *pistis*, introduced as patterns of imitation, is unthinkable in any Greek tradition."[7] William L. Lane explains that "the reason for this is that to the formally educated person, πίστις, 'faith,' was regarded as a state of mind characteristic of the uneducated, who believe something on hearsay without being able to give precise reasons for their belief. The willingness of Jews and Christians to suffer for the undemonstrable astonished pagan observers."[8]

What is *faith*?
Hebrews 11:1 provides a definition of *faith*: "Faith is the assurance [*hypostasis*] of things hoped for, the conviction [*elenchos*] of things not seen." The English Standard Version, which I just quoted, suggests that faith is an attitude: to believe is to be sure of the things you hope to receive or achieve and convinced about the things you cannot see. The problem with this translation is that the term *hypostasis*, translated as "assurance," did not refer in the time of Hebrews to an attitude but to a tangible reality. In other words, *hypostasis* did not originally refer to my feelings or my frame of mind but to reality and to what is independent of my frame of mind. In fact, philosophers used the term *hypostasis* to refer to reality as opposed to appearance.[9]

For example, one way *hypostasis* was used was to refer to the "guarantee of ownership" or "title deed" of something. Therefore, to have *hypostasis* regarding a property did not mean that you were *sure* or that you were *convinced* that the property was yours but that you had, in fact, the *title deed* of the property. Similarly, the term *elenchos*, used in the second half of the verse, did not mean "conviction" but "proof." Thus, both halves of Hebrews 11:1 use terms and ideas that agree with each other. According to the original sense of the words in this verse, faith does not have to do with feelings or a frame of mind but with reality and proof.

Several years ago, my father bought a house in which he lived happily for a few years. One day, a neighbor, who had just built a house next door to him, came to his house and told him that the fence around my father's house infringed on his property. My father was surprised by the claim. He had bought the house and the property from a friend who had also built the house. When my father checked with the county's records office, he found out that the neighbor was right. The builder had made a mistake and had built a section of the fence beyond the property line. Thankfully, the house itself was within the property lines. To believe, be sure, or be convinced that something is yours does not make it yours. Belief does not produce reality. Only the opposite is true. To have the *title deed* of a property does produce conviction and assurance. Proof provides assurance, but assurance does not provide proof.

The Holman Christian Standard Bible provides a better translation of Hebrews 11:1: "Now faith is the reality [*hypostasis*] of what is hoped for, the proof [*elenchos*] of what is not seen." This translation, though correct, creates its own set of problems. Is Hebrews saying that faith *is* reality—faith *is* proof?

Faith is reality; faith is proof

As I thought about my son's question, "Dad, how do you really know that Jesus is going to come back again?" I realized that faith is a phenomenon that has several different aspects.

First, I believe Jesus is going to come back again because He put that faith in me. I did not produce it. It came from above. Faith is a gift that comes from God and Christ (Romans 12:3; Ephesians 2:8,

9; 6:23, 24; Philippians 1:29). I heard about the promises of God in the sermons my father preached when I was a child. Those promises grabbed my heart. I had to insist several times and study a twenty-lesson baptismal course twice before I was allowed to be baptized. The Word of God has power. It elicits faith (Romans 10:17). Faith is based on and reveals the reality of God because it is God who produces it.

Second, and most importantly, faith is a form of evidence. When God promised that He would come a second time to save those who were waiting for Him, He gave them the Holy Spirit as a guarantee. The apostle Paul says that the promises of God are certain because He has guaranteed them by giving us the Holy Spirit (2 Corinthians 1:22; see also 5:5; Ephesians 1:14). The Greek word for "guarantee" is *arrabōn*, referring to a payment in advance of part of a purchase price to secure a legal claim to the object in question.[10] It is a down payment that provides legal assurance for the article desired. The curious thing is that it is God who is giving a pledge or guarantee that He will be faithful to His promises, not us.

The Holy Spirit functions as a down payment of God's promises in amazing ways. God's promises of salvation to those who believe in Him include the provision that He will resurrect them with an imperishable body,[11] transform the bodies of those who are alive,[12] and give both groups eternal life.[13] Hebrews tells us, however, that we have begun to taste today the powers of the age to come (Hebrews 6:4, 5). God has given us a down payment on these future realities through the Holy Spirit. Therefore, we have experienced a spiritual resurrection,[14] a renewed mind,[15] and a taste of eternal life in Christ.[16] The fruit of the Spirit—love, joy, peace, patience, kindness, goodness, faithfulness, gentleness, and self-control—are attributes of life in the new world, given to us as a first installment of the joys of eternal life. When the Holy Spirit dwells in me, I am already experiencing some aspects of what heaven will be like. Faith is part of that divine pledge.

Why, then, do I believe that Jesus will come again? Well, because

God has begun to fulfill His promises in my life today. I was given new life and was transformed by His power. I breathe the atmosphere of heaven even when surrounded by difficulties. That experience of faith through the Spirit is just a taste of what is coming soon. It is evidence that God is my Father and assures me that He will return soon to take me home (Romans 8:16; Galatians 4:6, 7). The title deed gives me assurance and a legal claim to the world to come (Ephesians 1:14).

How do we get faith?

The problem is that faith as reality and proof only makes sense to those who experience it. "The natural person does not accept the things of the Spirit of God, for they are folly to him, and he is not able to understand them because they are spiritually discerned" (1 Corinthians 2:14).

Faith is a gift of God, but it is not imposed. It has to be accepted. God always takes the first step. He does it for everyone who comes into this world (John 1:9). In the end, a lack of faith is the inability or unwillingness to recognize what God has done for us. In Hebrews, the desert generation is the prime example of a lack of faith (Hebrews 3:7–19). When they came to the border of the Promised Land, they lost nerve. They became afraid of the giants and the fortified cities, and they thought they would never conquer the land. Their problem was not that they were afraid but that they forgot how God had delivered them from the Egyptian army, opened the Red Sea, and provided for all of their needs. They forgot that God was with them in the cloud to guide and protect them. Their lack of faith was the tragic result of a misplaced focus and of forgetfulness. We do not build faith through exercises of bravery and promises kept. We build faith by keeping our minds on what God has done and is doing for us.

I do not remember everything I said to my son when he asked why I knew that Jesus was coming again. Whatever it was, it does not matter now because it did not make sense to him then. In the aftermath of that dark moment, my wife and I entered into a fight with God. We had come to the end of our rope. We had nowhere to go.

Only God could reach across the pain and the darkness and reveal Himself to my son.

We continued praying for two years, attended church every Sabbath, read the Bible at home every day, related how God had loved and provided for us in the past, and held onto God as best we could. It was a long wait, but finally, God came through. One morning, Hadid told me with a smile on his face: "Dad, do you know what happened yesterday?"

"No," I answered.

"Jesus was standing at the foot of my bed." This was especially significant because Hadid suffered from sleep terrors. This was the first of two interventions by God that started him on a journey that restored faith in a little boy whose sorrow did not let him see God. Today, Hadid works as a pastor for the Seventh-day Adventist Church in the New Jersey Conference. What a God we serve!

---

1. This paragraph is quoted from Félix H. Cortez, "Creation in Hebrews," in *The Genesis Creation Account and Its Reverberations in the New Testament*, ed. Thomas Shepherd (Berrien Springs, MI: Andrews University Press, 2021).

2. E. R. Dodds, *Pagan and Christian in an Age of Anxiety* (Cambridge, UK: Cambridge University Press, 1965), 121.

3. Dodds, *Pagan and Christian*, 121.

4. Dodds, 121.

5. Dodds, 121.

6. Dodds, 121.

7. James W. Thompson, *The Beginnings of Christian Philosophy: The Epistle to the Hebrews* (Washington, DC: Catholic Biblical Association of America, 1982), 53.

8. William L. Lane, *Hebrews 9–13*, Word Biblical Commentary, vol. 47B (Grand Rapids, MI: Zondervan, 1991), 316. See also Dodds, *Pagan and Christian*, 120–122.

9. Luke Timothy Johnson, *Hebrews: A Commentary* (Louisville, KY: Westminster John Knox, 2006), 277.

10. Frederick W. Danker, Walter Bauer, William F. Arndt, and F. Wilbur Gingrich, *Greek-English Lexicon of the New Testament and Other Early Christian Literature*, 3rd ed. (Chicago: University of Chicago Press, 2000), 134.

11. John 5:28, 29; 1 Thessalonians 4:16.

12. 1 Corinthians 15:51, 52; Philippians 3:21.

13. Matthew 25:46; Luke 18:30.

14. Ephesians 2:5, 6; Colossians 2:12, 13; 3:1.
15. Romans 12:2; Titus 3:5.
16. John 5:24; 1 John 5:11, 12.

Twelve

Receiving an Unshakable Kingdom

In general, people do not like to endure a trial or a judgment procedure unless they need to defend their rights or seek vindication from accusations made against them. One of my favorite cousins once went to court to defend herself. She had been ticketed for not wearing a seat belt, but she felt the citation was excessive because of extenuating circumstances. She challenged the ticket, and a court date was set. But when the day arrived, my cousin forgot the appointment and failed to attend the court hearing. When she realized what had happened, she was distressed and asked me to pray for her. Though she was able to secure a second date, the court had made it clear that it was not pleased. That night my wife and I knelt to intercede before God in prayer. "Lord," I said, "help my cousin so that the judge will be fair with her."

As soon as I finished praying, before we got up, my wife blurted out: "Fair? What she needs is that the judge be merciful with her, not fair!" She was right, so we prayed again.

Throughout Adventist history, many have challenged the biblical teaching of the pre-Advent, or investigative, judgment.[1] The pre-Advent judgment refers to the second phase of the high priestly ministry of

Jesus in heaven that began in 1844, fulfilling the prophecies of Daniel 7 and 8. For these people, judgment is contrary to the gospel. Challengers to this doctrine have often used the letter to the Hebrews as one of their main arguments. For example, Desmond Ford, one of the most recent and significant challengers to this teaching, argued that he could not find an allusion to Daniel or any reference to a two-phase ministry of Jesus in the heavenly sanctuary.[2]

Judgment, however, is very important in the argument of Hebrews. The author constantly reminds his readers that a judgment is coming and that they need to prepare.[3] The purpose of this chapter is to explore the teaching in Hebrews of the judgment and its support of the pre-Advent judgment of Daniel 7.[4] It is also the purpose of this chapter to explain why the pre-Advent, or investigative, judgment is good news for us.

The allusions to Haggai 2 and Daniel 7 in Hebrews

An *allusion* is a way to talk about a hermeneutical strategy. What I mean by this is that authors often refer to a person, a thing, an event, an idea, or a place to give their readers the key to understanding what they are trying to say. For example, if I tell my wife that our neighbor was a good Samaritan and helped me clear the snow out of the driveway, I want her to use the story of the good Samaritan as a key to interpret or understand what the neighbor's help meant to me.

Non-Adventist biblical scholars have pointed out that Hebrews 12:28 is probably an allusion to Daniel 7:18.[5] The passage says, "Therefore, since we are receiving a kingdom which cannot be shaken, let us have grace, by which we may serve God acceptably with reverence and godly fear" (Hebrews 12:28, NKJV). In biblical literature, the idea that believers, the people of God, are receiving a kingdom that cannot be destroyed or will remain forever is unique to Daniel 7.[6] Note the following important verbal connections.

"But the **saints of the Most High** shall RECEIVE the KINGDOM, and possess the kingdom *forever, even forever and ever*" (Daniel 7:18, NKJV).

Therefore, since **we** ARE RECEIVING a KINGDOM which *cannot be shaken*, let us have grace (Hebrews 12:28, NKJV).

Both passages talk about a kingdom that is received by believers ("the saints"). Furthermore, both passages affirm that the kingdom cannot be destroyed. It will last forever. The only difference is that what is future in Daniel is described as present in Hebrews.

There are several reasons why Hebrews 12:28 is likely an allusion to Daniel 7:18. First, it is clear that the author knew the story of Daniel. Hebrews 11:33, 34 refers to Daniel's rescue from the mouths of the lions[7] and probably to his friends being rescued from the fiery furnace.[8]

Second, early Christians were clearly acquainted with the book of Daniel and with the prophecy of Daniel 7 specifically. The book of Daniel is cited frequently in Jewish apocalyptic literature that existed before or during the time of the New Testament.[9] Daniel is referred to many times in the New Testament. In fact, Matthew 24:15 refers to Daniel by name. Scholars have suggested that more than 150 passages in the New Testament allude to the book of Daniel,[10] which is significant given that Daniel is not a large book. Most importantly, many of the allusions (around a third of the total) are to Daniel 7. In fact, the clearest allusions to Daniel in the New Testament are to Daniel 7:13.[11] The Apostolic Fathers, who lived in the second century AD, quote Daniel at least six times and three of which are from Daniel 7.[12] It is clear, then, that the prophecy of Daniel 7 was an important text for New Testament authors and the early Christian church.

Third, the immediate context of Hebrews 12 also suggests that the author had Daniel 7 in mind. Daniel 7 describes a judgment scene before an "Ancient of Days," where "ten thousand times ten thousand" stand before Him and where the books are opened. The result of the judgment is that "the saints of the Most High shall receive the king-dom and possess the kingdom forever, forever and ever" (Daniel 7:18). Similarly, Hebrews 12:22–24 describes a joyous judgment scene at Mount Zion, the heavenly Jerusalem. Believers who are enrolled in books in heaven and "innumerable angels"[13] come before God, the Judge of all. They also come to Jesus, who mediates a new covenant in their favor.

After describing this joyous judgment scene, the author warns believers that they need to pay attention to what God is saying to them because God will once more shake heaven and the earth so that every-thing that can be shaken may be removed (Hebrews 12:25–27). This shaking of heaven is a reference to the prophecy of Haggai 2. Those who "remain" will receive "a kingdom that cannot be shaken" (Hebrews 12:27, 28). Thus, the reference to the shaking of heaven, predicted in Haggai 2, is followed by the reference to the saints receiv-ing the kingdom, which was predicted in Daniel 7.

It is important to note that Matthew 24:29, 30 and Luke 21:26, 27 allude to the shaking of Haggai 2:6 and to the reception of the king-dom in Daniel 7 in the same order they appear in Hebrews 12:25–28. The author of Hebrews has given us, then, the prophecies of Haggai 2 and Daniel 7 as a hermeneutical key to understanding the passage of Hebrews 12:22–29.

The purpose of the pre-Advent judgment
You may wonder why the judgment scene of Hebrews 12:22–24 is joyous. It certainly does not fit the gloomy vision that some Adventists have developed about the pre-Advent judgment—a time in which believers appear alone to be scrutinized before the judgment seat of an Almighty and Holy God and a retinue of innumerable angels. The truth is that the gloomy view of the pre-Advent judgment does not fit the prophecies of Daniel 7 and 8 or the prophecies of Revelation either. In the prophecies of Daniel 7 and 8, the judgment is carried out to deliver the saints from the attacks of the little horn and restore

them to God's kingdom. In the prophecies of Revelation, the saints cry out to God, desperate for Him to begin the judgment (Revelation 6:9–11). Later on, the judgment is announced as the good news of the gospel (Revelation 14:6, 7). Similarly, the announcement in Haggai 2:6, 7, 21, 22 that God will shake heaven and the earth is considered good news for the people of God.

The reference to the shaking of heaven and earth in Hebrews 12:25–27 is very significant. In the Old Testament, the shaking of the earth is a common occurrence when God shows up to deliver His people. When Deborah and Barak fought against King Jabin of Canaan and Sisera, the commander of his army, God fought from heaven on their behalf (Judges 5:20). This is described as a powerful earthquake, a shaking of the earth and mountains, because of the presence of the Lord (verses 4, 5). This same image appears throughout the Old Testament when God appears to deliver the oppressed.[14] Thus, shaking becomes a signal of God's judgment on the oppressors.[15] In the Prophets, it happens in the context of the day of the Lord.[16]

Similarly, Haggai promised that God would "shake the heavens and the earth . . . and all the nations" and fill the temple with glory by bringing the nations' treasures to the temple they were building (Haggai 2:6–9). He explained this in oracles pronounced two months later, on the twenty-fourth of the ninth month (520 BC; Haggai 2:10–23). The oracles explain that the Lord would overthrow the kingdoms and their armies and then establish His own king in Jerusalem, from the line of David (represented by Zerubbabel), giving Him total authority, like that represented by a signet ring (verse 23). The purpose of the judgments predicted in the prophecies of Daniel 7 and Haggai 2 is then favorable for the people of God because they have the purpose of delivering His people from their enemies.

The nature of the pre-Advent judgment
It is important to note that when God appears to judge the wicked, the people of God must not be counted among the wicked if they want to

111

be delivered. According to the Old Testament, only the righteous are not destroyed, or "shaken." If they are to be delivered, the people of God must be free from sin, having steadfast love for God and putting their trust in Him.[17]

But we will not understand the nature of the judgment in Hebrews unless we understand that Hebrews considers this promised "shaking" to be a second judgment: "Yet *once more* I will shake not only the earth but also the heavens" (Hebrews 12:26; emphasis added). From the perspective of Hebrews, the first judgment was in the past. The second one was yet to come.

The first "shaking," or judgment, happened at the cross and tells us about the nature of the pre-Advent judgment. The work of Jesus as King and Priest in the heavenly sanctuary occurs in two phases. At the cross, Jesus destroyed the power of the devil, who had the power of death (Hebrews 2:14–16, NIV). Satan lived on, but his power was broken. Hebrews 1:13 and 10:12, 13 say that Jesus is now seated at the right hand of God, waiting for the time when Satan will be made a footstool. Thus, the Cross was the first shaking, and the second shaking will be during the end-time events that will culminate with the destruction of the devil and the wicked in the lake of fire (Revelation 20:7–15).[18]

Similarly, as Priest, Jesus died on the cross and ascended to heaven to appear before God and claim the benefits of His sacrifice in our favor in order to redeem us from our transgressions (Hebrews 9:15–26). His work of salvation has not finished yet, however. Jesus will appear a second time to save those who are eagerly waiting for Him (verses 27, 28).

The Cross was, then, the first shaking and the first stage of judgment. When Jesus died, the earth shook, the veil of the temple was torn in two, tombs were opened, and many saints were resurrected (Matthew 27:51–53). Jesus referred to this event as the judgment of this world and the moment Satan was cast out from heaven (John 12:31; 16:8–11; Revelation 12:3–12). Paul calls this event the firstfruits of a larger resurrection that will occur in the future (1 Corinthians 15:20–28). Therefore, we are now at the border of the fulfillment of the second stage of the judgment—the second shaking. We are close to the time when God will consummate His promises for His people so that they can enter into the Promised Land (Hebrews 10:35–39). This is indeed a time of great joy and expectation for the people of God. The court has been set, and the judgment is ready to begin.

The intimate relationship that exists between the two phases is very important. They depend on each other. Without the Cross, there cannot be a Second Coming. Without the Second Coming, the promise of the Cross remains unfulfilled. The judgment is a two-pole system. If you take one out, you destroy the system. That is why believers cannot face the judgment as if the Cross did not exist. Those who envision the final judgment as a moment in which they will appear alone before God so that their actions can be scrutinized miss the point. The purpose of the judgment is to find out who has benefited from Christ's sacrifice. Those who have embraced Christ or, as Paul said elsewhere, are "in Christ" are perfect. They are righteous. If we are "in Christ," we will not be shaken because Christ cannot be shaken. If the earthquake does not topple the trunk, it does not knock over the branches. The question is not how strong the earthquake is but how strong the trunk is.

In the case of my beloved cousin, there was a dilemma between justice and mercy. In the case of the final judgment, this dilemma does not exist. God will be both fully righteous and totally merciful. This is possible because of Christ. When we abandon ourselves to follow Him, when we hand Him complete control over our lives, He becomes our Representative. We are clothed with the righteousness of Christ, and His robe of righteousness will withstand all scrutiny.

A thorough judgment will bring glory to Jesus. It will show the universe what Jesus did for us at the cross and in us throughout our lives. Jesus, His work, and His accomplishments will forever be the center of attention. I believe that during the pre-Advent judgment, there will be repeated standing ovations for Jesus, celebrating His victories as He represents His people.

---

1. See Frank B. Holbrook, ed., *Doctrine of the Sanctuary: A Historical Survey (1845–1863),* Daniel and Revelation Committee Series 5 (Silver Spring, MD: Biblical Research Institute, 1989), 197–216.

2. Holbrook, *Doctrine of the Sanctuary*, 218.

3. Hebrews 2:1–4; 4:12, 13; 6:1, 2, 7, 8; 9:27, 28; 10:24, 25, 30, 31; 12:25–29.

4. For a deeper and more detailed analysis, see Félix H. Cortez, " 'Shaking the Heavens and the Earth': Daniel and the Eschatology of Hebrews," in *Eschatology From an Adventist Perspective: Proceedings of the Fourth International Bible Conference, Rome, June 11–20, 2018*, ed. Elias Brasil de Souza, A. Rahel Wells, Laszlo Gallusz, and Denis Kaiser (Silver Spring, MD: Biblical Research Institute, 2021) 201–222.

5. See the marginal reading to Hebrews 12:28 in Kurt Aland, Barbara Aland, and Johannes Karavidopoulos, eds., *Novum Testamentum Graece*, 28th ed. (Stuttgart: Deutsche Bibelgesellschaft, 2012). See also major commentaries on Hebrews.

6. Similar but more limited ideas are found in Luke 12:32; 19:12.

7. Daniel 6:23.

8. Alluding to Daniel 3:25.

9. See G. K. Beale, *The Use of Daniel in Jewish Apocalyptic Literature and in the Revelation of St. John* (Lanham, MD: University Press of America, 1984).

10. See Aland, Aland, and Karavidopoulos, *Novum Testamentum Graece*, 865, 866.

11. Daniel 7:13 is clearly referred to in Matthew 24:30; 26:64; Mark 14:62; Luke 21:27; Revelation 1:7; 14:14.

12. 1 Clement 34:6 (Daniel 7:10); 1 Clement 45:6 (Daniel 6:16); 1 Clement 45:7 (Daniel 3:19–21); Barnabas 4:4 (Daniel 7:24); Barnabas 4:5 (Daniel 7:7, 8); Barnabas 16:6 (Daniel 9:24).

13. Literally, "ten thousands."

14. Psalms 10:6; 46:5, 6; 60:2; 68:7, 8; 77:17, 18; 97:4; 107:27; Micah 1:4; Nahum 1:5; Habakkuk 3:6. Similarly, Matthew 24:29; Mark 13:25; Luke 21:26; cf. Acts 16:26.

15. In fact, shaking (*saleuō*) means "judgment" in LXX (2 Kings 17:20; Psalm 47:6, 7 [48:5, 6, Masoretic Text]; Lamentations 1:8).

16. Isaiah 13:13; 24:18–23; Ezekiel 38:19–23; Joel 2:10, 11; Habakkuk 3:6, 16.

17. Psalms 15:5; 16:8; 21:7; 62:2; 112:6.

18. These final events include the pre-Advent judgment, the Second Coming, the millennium, and the judgment after the millennium.

Thirteen

Let Brotherly Love Continue

Hebrews closes with suggestions of how the teachings it has presented throughout the epistle should be applied in the practical life of the readers. For the apostle Paul, the probable author, theology had to have a practical expression, and so it should be for us as well. Thus, the apostle suggests at the end of his epistle that the main teachings of his letters about Jesus' rule and intercession at the right hand of God in the heavenly sanctuary should be expressed through brotherly love among believers.

The author does not see the audience as a group of individuals who work on their salvation in a one-to-one relationship with Jesus but as a family, or household, that is being saved together or is traveling together to the heavenly homeland. Believers are brothers of one another.[1] They belong to the household of the High Priest Jesus.[2] Jesus is also the Firstborn, the Elder Brother who models to believers how they should treat each other, and their co-heir.[3] On this basis, the author has repeatedly admonished the readers to exhort, encourage, and watch for one another.[4]

Brotherly love was an ideal well attested in the Greek world, Judaism, and the New Testament.[5] Scholars have suggested that "the relationship between siblings was the closest, strongest, and most intimate of relationships in the ancient world."[6] For example, Aristotle said that brothers were, in a sense, "the same thing, though separate individuals."[7] Similarly, Plutarch said that brothers "become united in their emotions and actions, and share with each other their studies and recreations and games." "[Siblings] use in common a parent's wealth and friends and slaves . . . [in the manner that] a single soul would make use of the hands and feet and eyes of two bodies."[8]

Hebrews presents Jesus as the greatest example of brotherly love. Jesus was not ashamed to be identified with the human race. Instead, He shared their condition,[9] announced and praised God's name to them,[10] suffered with them and for them,[11] and now leads them into glory[12] where they will share His inheritance.[13] Therefore, the author now exhorts the readers to follow the example of Jesus in loving one another and taking care of one another as Jesus took care of them.

According to Hebrews 13, brotherly love should be expressed in at least six, or perhaps, seven forms: hospitality (verse 2), visiting and supporting prisoners and those who had been mistreated (verse 3; probably the same group), honoring marriage (verse 4), avoiding covetousness (verses 5, 6), remembering and obeying the leaders of the congregation (verses 7–17), and praying for the author himself (verses 18, 19). Of all these elements, I will focus on the following two: hospitality and remembering and obeying the leaders of the congregation.

Do not neglect to show hospitality

The first way in which believers must show brotherly love is through hospitality. The author reminds his readers that by entertaining strangers, "some have unwittingly entertained angels" (Hebrews 13:2, NKJV).[14] This is, in fact, an understatement. Abraham and Sarah hosted the Lord Himself.[15] Please note that the author exhorts believers to show hospitality not because that is the right thing to do or because that is one way to honor God or to emulate Jesus. The author suggests that providing hospitality is in the best interest of the host.

I grew up in a home with a strong tradition of hospitality. We lived most of the time near important education centers for our Adventist community, and as a result, there were young people living in our home almost all the time. Sometimes they were relatives, but in the majority of cases, they were not. As I think about it, I realize that we have been the greatest beneficiaries. We acquired many friends from many different places who have made our lives richer. More intriguingly, however, I have been the object of amazing hospitality by others. I graduated as a pastor when I was twenty years old and began to work immediately as an associate pastor in Toluca, Mexico. At that time, the family of Alejandro and Libia Rivera opened their home to me. They had in their home a room on the third floor where I lived for six months. They became my family. Nira, Ale, and Libni, who were very young at the time, became my little sisters. They told me that the room would be my room whenever I wanted to return. And I would return from time to time to introduce them to my wife and then to my kids as they were born. Thirty years later, we still talk on the phone now and then. This is not the only case; many other families provided incredible hospitality during my first years of ministry.[16] How do you repay that? The best thing you can do, I think, is provide hospitality to others. I think that God's dream is that the Adventist Church becomes truly a worldwide extended family.

This is what happened in the early church. Early Christians were, indeed, a big family. They shared with one another everything they had (Acts 4:32–37). This was not a short-lived attitude resulting from the fervor of a novel experience. Hospitality became part of the ethos of Christianity. An early Christian document from the beginning of the second century AD, called the Didache, provided instructions to help churches avoid abuse by charlatans while still affirming and encouraging hospitality (chapters 11–13). Similarly, Lucian, in a satire from the second century, referred to the hospitality of Christians: "Their first lawgiver persuaded them that they are all brothers of one another. . . . Therefore they despise all things [i.e., material goods] indiscriminately and consider them common property."[17] Helping those who were in prison was an important aspect of hospitality. Most prisoners depended on relatives or friends to provide for their food and needs. Those who remembered and provided material support to Christians in jail also provided important emotional support. They became "partners" with them, making themselves vulnerable to social abuse (Hebrews 10:33, 34). Thus, Ignatius of Antioch, who was taken prisoner to Rome during the first years of the second century AD and was greeted and supported by church members in the cities along the route, testified: "My life is a humble offering for you; and so are these chains of mine, for which you never showed the least contempt or shame. Neither will Jesus Christ in His perfect loyalty show Himself ashamed of you."[18] Lucian, in his satire, also attested to the care of Christians for those in prison:

> The Christians . . . left nothing undone in the effort to rescue [Peregrinus]. Then, as this was impossible, every other form of attention was shown him. . . . From the very break of day aged widows and orphan children could be seen waiting near the prison, while their officials even slept inside with him after bribing the guards. Then elaborate meals were brought in, and sacred books of theirs were read aloud. . . .
>
> Indeed, people came even from the cities in Asia, sent by the Christians at their common expense, to succour and defend and encourage the hero. They show incredible speed whenever any such public action is taken; for in no time they lavish their all.[19]

The support early Christians gave to those in prison was a token of the support Jesus Himself had promised: He would "never leave . . . nor forsake" them (Hebrews 13:5).

Hospitality and help for those in prison continued among Christians for a long time. Early in the fourth century AD, Pachomius was swept up by the Roman army as a forced recruit when he was around twenty years old and was held in captivity. He was very saddened by this, but a group of local Christians came to console him and provide help for him and his companions and treated them very well. Pachomius had been born in a pagan home and apparently knew very little about Christians, but he was deeply moved by their example and vowed to devote his life to serve others. After his release, he inquired about Christianity and converted. He later became one of the principal founders of cenobitic monasticism. ("Cenobitic" comes from the Greek words *koinos* [common] and *bios* [life] and refers to monastic life in a community.) By the time of his death, he had founded nine monasteries for men and two for women. In these monasteries, spiritual exercises were combined with manual work for the benefit of the poor.

Remember your leaders

The longest element of brotherly love in Hebrews 13 (verses 7–17) refers to respect and obedience toward the leaders of the congregation. It begins with an invitation to "remember" those leaders of the past who spoke "the word of God" to them and closes with a call to "obey" the leaders in the present because they "watch out" for you (verses 7, 17, NKJV). Those leaders of the past are most likely those who first preached the Word to them and founded the congregation. The call to remember them does not simply refer to a mental exercise of recollection nor to an external tribute honoring them. The author explains that they are to "remember" them by "considering the outcome of their conduct" (verse 7, NKJV) and by imitating their faith. In this way, the author has added the founding leaders of the congregation to the list of faithful heroes of Hebrews 11 whom believers should emulate. For the author, the greatest act of remembrance and praise is emulation.

Believers are exhorted to obey the leaders because "they are keeping watch over your souls" (verse 17). The leaders of the congregation are described here as pastors who are in charge of the spiritual well-being of their flock and who will give "an account" to God for their spiritual state.[20] The context suggests that these leaders are undershepherds who serve under Jesus, "the great Shepherd of the sheep" (verse 20, NASB). The result of care and faithfulness among the leaders and obedience or trust among the members of the congregation will be joy. The phrase could be read in the sense that the leaders will be able to serve the congregation with "joy"[21] or that they will give an account of the congregation under their care in the final judgment "with joy and not with groaning" (verse 17).[22]

One of the important functions of the leaders is to protect the congregation from false doctrines. The author refers to this when he exhorts them, "Do not be led away by diverse and strange teachings, for it is good for the heart to be strengthened by grace, not by foods, which have not benefited those devoted to them" (verse 9). The author does not explain what these teachings were or what kind of foods he was talking about. The author is probably not referring to the distinction between clean and unclean. We know from Acts 10 and 15:7–29 that the early Christian church did not consider the distinction between clean and unclean foods contrary to the gospel. Furthermore, it is difficult to see how abstaining from unclean foods would establish, or strengthen, the "heart" (Hebrews 13:9). The context suggests that the author is not criticizing the audience for abstaining from certain foods but for participating in eating them with the hope of obtaining some spiritual benefits.

The author is probably referring to participating in sacrifices in the temple or in ritual or cultic meals that were considered to provide some spiritual benefit. The Old Testament considered the sacrifices to be "food offerings" to God (Leviticus 21:6, 8, 17), and Malachi 1:7, 12 referred to the altar as the "Lord's table." Thus, it is not strange that the author related the "gifts and sacrifices" of the old covenant to "foods and drinks" in Hebrews 9:9, 10 (NKJV). The apostle may also be referring to cultic meals that Jews, especially diaspora Jews, celebrated as an extension of the sacrifices in the Jewish temple in

Jerusalem. Josephus provides evidence that diaspora Jews observed special sacrificial mealtimes in connection or imitation of the fellowship sacrifice meals at the temple, which were called *syndeipna* ("fellowship meals").[23] This is probably what the author of Hebrews objected to. Grace is not mediated through sacrifices at the temple or through fellowship meals that imitate and depend on the altar in the temple but through the sacrifice and priestly mediation of Jesus Christ. The "diverse and strange teachings" refer, then, to means of blessing that do not have their origin in Christ.

"Let us go to him outside the camp"

According to Israel's legislation in the desert, those who were impure were cast out of the camp because God was within the camp and unwilling to see any "unclean" or "indecent" thing (*aschēmosynē*).[24] Thus, biblical legislation presupposed that the presence of God was within the camp. Thus, when Jesus endured the cross, He was cast outside the camp as a "shameful," "unclean," or "indecent" thing (*aischynēs*).[25] The apostle's exhortation in Hebrews 13:13 suggests, however, that God's presence is now outside the camp. The action of going to Jesus outside the camp means not only "bearing His reproach," or shame (verse 12, NKJV) but also going "forth to Him," just as those Israelites who "sought the LORD" went "outside the camp" in the desert when Moses removed God's tent from the camp after the golden calf controversy (Exodus 33:7).

The greatest respect and obedience that Christians can offer toward their leaders is their emulation of the example of Jesus Christ. The author exhorts believers to follow the path Jesus traveled, who went outside the camp, despising the shame of the cross.[26] This was also the path Moses followed. He chose to bear "the reproach of Christ" instead of the treasures of Egypt (Hebrews 11:26). The apostle's exhortation here is the same as we find in the Gospels to take up our cross and follow Jesus.[27] The exclusion from the camp, both for Jesus and His followers, implies shame.

Going outside the camp is a painful experience but sometimes unavoidable when we follow Jesus. At the beginning of my ministry, I had the sad experience of seeing a group of believers who had to leave their congregation in order to remain faithful to Jesus. That Adventist congregation had been taken over by leadership that rejected the conference's authority and retained part of the tithes for local use. I was the director of the Youth Department at the time, but the conference asked me to make a Sabbath morning presentation on the use of the tithe. When we arrived, the leaders prevented us from speaking to the church, and a group of people demanded loudly that we leave the premises. It was a sad moment. We had to stand and leave, but a group of congregation members followed us, and we met in the house of a church member who lived nearby. They went out of the camp to follow Jesus. For years, they endured the inconvenience of not having a proper temple to meet in but remained faithful, and Jesus did not disappoint them. Today, the temple has been recovered, fellowship has been restored, and there are now two congregations in the place of one.

It may be possible that circumstances force us to leave our jobs, our communities, or even our families to remain faithful to Jesus. When we do that, when we are reproached for loyalty to our Savior, we emulate and honor the One who left behind everything to save us. And when believers do that, Jesus stands in heaven to honor them.[28]

---

1. Hebrews 3:1, 12; 10:19; 13:22.
2. Hebrews 3:6; 10:21.
3. Hebrews 1:2, 4, 14; 6:17; 9:15.
4. Hebrews 3:12, 13; 10:24, 25; 12:12–17.
5. Greek world: Plutarch, *On Brotherly Love* [*Moralia* 478B–492D]; Lucian, *Dialogues of the Dead* 26. Judaism: 4 Maccabees 13:23, 26; 14:1; Philo, *Embassy* 87; Josephus, *Jewish Antiquities* 2.161; 4.26; 12.189. New Testament: Romans 12:10; 1 Thessalonians 4:9; 1 Peter 1:22; 2 Peter 1:7.
6. David A. deSilva, *Perseverance in Gratitude* (Grand Rapids, MI: Eerdmans, 2000), 486.
7. Aristotle, *Nicomachean Ethics* 1161b30–35.
8. Plutarch, *On Brotherly Love* [*Moralia* 478C–D].
9. Hebrews 2:14.

10. Hebrews 2:11, 12.

11. Hebrews 2:9, 10, 14–18.

12. Hebrews 2:10; 3:1; 4:14–16; 6:19, 20; 10:19–25; 12:1–3.

13. Hebrews 1:2, 4, 14; 6:17; 9:15.

14. Genesis 19:1–14; Judges 6:11–14.

15. Genesis 18:12–15.

16. The Leon family, the Yepez family, the Marroquin family, and others.

17. Lucian, *The Passing of Peregrinus* 13, ed. T. E. Page et al., trans. A. M. Harmon, Loeb Classical Library 5 (Cambridge, MA: Harvard University Press, 1962), 15.

18. Ignatius, *To the Smyrnaeans* 10.

19. Lucian, *Passing of Peregrinus* 12 (Loeb Classical Library), 13–15.

20. Cf. 1 Peter 5:1–4; 1 Corinthians 3:10–15.

21. E.g., Romans 16:19; 2 Corinthians 2:3; 7:16.

22. E.g., Philippians 2:16; 1 Corinthians 3:10–15.

23. Josephus, *Jewish Antiquities* 14.189, 213–215, 257, 260, 261.

24. Numbers 5:3; Deuteronomy 23:14, LXX.

25. Hebrews 12:2.

26. Hebrews 12:2; 13:12, 13.

27. Mark 8:34; Matthew 10:38; 16:24; Luke 14:27; cf. Galatians 2:20.

28. Acts 7:56; Luke 12:8.

Notes

Notes

Notes

Notes

Notes